Reluctant Fathers

Son of a Muslim League leader speaks

By

Shahinul Islam Khalisdar

Contents

About the Book	4
Introduction	5
The Bengal	**8**
Hinduism	10
Buddhism	13
1202 War	13
Muslim	15
Muslim Sultanate	**24**
Shia Rule	26
East India Company Rules	29
The Battle of Plassey	31
Hindu Zamindars	33
British Rule	35
Lord Curzon	36
Partition of Bengal	37
Bengali Nationalism	40
Muslim League	43
Sher E Bengal	50
Khwaja Nazimuddin	52
Huseyn Shaheed Suhrawardy	53
Jinnah	**54**
Pakistan	56
President Ayub Khan	61

Mujib	64
1970 Election	65
The 1971 War	67
Countdown to The 71 War	**72**
All Parties Roundtable Meetings	73
President Ayub Khan Resign	74
General Yahya Khan's Presidency & War 71	75
Cyclone Bhola 1970	76
1970 General Elections	77
Flag Hoisted	80
7th March Speech	81
Searchlight Operation March 25	82
The Serajul Alam Khan's War	**86**
Declaration of Independence	88
Bangladesh Government	89
The War	90
Mukti Bahini	91
Mujib Bahini	91
Qader Bahini	92
Pro-Pakistani Elements	92
Al-Badr	93
Al-Shams	95
Islamic Jihad or Jundiin Muhammed	95
Peace Committee	95

Bangladesh	**97**
Bangladesh Economy	99
Conclusion	**104**

About the Book

Based on my childhood memories from bedtime stories from my Boro Ma, the Reluctant Fathers, my father's coffee table conversations with his friends, colleagues, and relatives, and my political discussion with some prominent political leaders and journalists from Bangladesh, India, and Pakistan during my Muslim Student activism in the Tri-States area. I do not belong to any political parties or their political ideology in Bangladesh or any part of the world. I am an independent USA citizen and simple ordinary Muslim born in a Muslim political family in Sylhet, Bangladesh. However, I am a grandson of a Muslim League founding member and son of a late Muslim League Leader that specific political background compels me to write this book. The Reluctant Fathers reflects the past political issues in the Indian subcontinent that I do not intend to hurt anyone's feelings or emotions. I intended to maintain an independent political perspective and neutrality free from political, religious, and cultural bias. Of course, I am a born Muslim and have gained Islamic knowledge in the Aqeedah throughout my life. I wrote from whatever I heard in my childhood and research found on youtube, Google, and public libraries to correlate to my hearing of Indian, Pakistani, and Bangladeshi political issues, actors, and events. I am confident this book is a practical and accurate historical political issue for Pakistan and Bangladesh.

Introduction

Since my toddler age, I have heard about the 1971 War. That war is a pride of Bangladeshi Bengali. It is one of the highest achievements Bangladeshi Bengali earned in their thousands of years of history. Bangladeshi Bengali call it "Hazar Bosorer Bengali.". Bangladeshi Bengalis are passionately argumentative to defend their Bengali identity and culture in restaurants, college cafeterias, and annual celebrations by cursing Razakars, al-Badr, al-shams. That makes it feel more Bengali than Indian Bengali as a whole.

On the other hand, the 1971 war was the greatest humiliation to the Muslim nationalist in the world. In thousands of years of Islamic History, Muslims never faced similar humiliation. Nearly ninety thousand well-trained militaries surrendered to the enemy and were taken as prisoners of war. As a grandson of Muslim League founding members and son of a Muslim League leader, I can sense it.

In reality, the 71 war was a successful military, intelligence, political, and foreign policy Indian victory. India bore the burden of millions of dollars smear campaign against Pakistan from (I.B. operation) 1948-1967 and (RAW operation) 1967-1971, a multibillion-dollar project for conventional war and guerrilla war training for defect Pakistani military officers and soldiers and recruited civilians for 1971 war. The foreign policy victory was realized when the USA refused to ship military supplies to East Pakistan and an air-force fleet. The political triumph recognized in 1972 Bangladesh wrote a constitution within the Indian doctrines.

I do respect Bangladeshi Bengalis' pridefulness in being Bengali. I am not entirely convinced of creating Pakistan in 1947. However, I was also born in Bangladesh. I have a thousand years of indigenous blood lineal in Sylhet that gave me the right to share my side of the analytical opinion. That's why I have decided to write "Reluctant Fathers." I am fully aware that Bangladeshi Bengali will viciously demonstrate their lowest behavior to insult my family and me. Nevertheless, I strongly feel that the grandsons of Muslim League founders can share their thought and historical count.

In 2006, I was in Iʿtikāf in Jamaica Muslim center, NYC. After completion of the Iʿtikāf, I came home and turned on the computer to check my email. I was shocked to see a couple of disturbing emails sent to me by some former Muslim student activists. In Bangladesh, Bengali Nationalists beating to death a Muslim activist, and thousands of Bengali by standard watched the brutally murdering an innocent man. The international media was silent. It needed to mention that I was writing a 32 pages book on a hundred years of failure of the Muslim League politics in the Indian subcontinent, Muslim League was created on 12/30/1906, and 2006 was exactly a hundred years. From that day, I deleted the Book and promised never to talk to Bengalis about Bangladeshi politics.

I do not intend to defend the Muslim League's Muslim Nationalism's politicization in the subcontinent and the two nations theory. I do not believe in coercion as Allah (SWT) said: "There is no compulsion in religion, the right direction distinguishes from the wrong." Al-Quran, 2:256. "I worship not that which you worship. Nor will you worship whom I worship. And I shall not worship that which you are worshipping. Nor will you worship that which I worship. To you be your religion and to me my religion. Al-Quran 109, 2-6. "For me are my deeds, and for you are your deeds! You are innocent of what I do, and I am innocent of what you do". Al-Quran 10:41.

This Book is comprehensive, direct, and straightforward to the political issues regarding Bangladesh and its people. And my personal opinions throughout the Book about the political actors and issue-based events. I did not intend to convince or convert anyone's belief about Bangladesh. Everyone is free to believe whatever they wish.

On YouTube, all the bloggers express their points of view according to their whimsical thinking. I intended to be free from bias and blindly defend anyone. The truth is one, and lies are ninety-nine. I will stick with the bedtime stories, my dad's coffee-table conversation, YouTube documentary video clips, and Quran and Sunnah.

The Bengal

I am briefly giving you the history of Bengal matching with the Hindu historians count. Hindu historians argue that Stone Age tools were found in the region, suggesting human habitation for over twenty thousand years. Remnants of Copper Age settlements, including pit dwellings, date back four thousand years. People were settling in Bengal identify as Austroasiatic, Tibeto-Burmans, Dravidians, and Indo-Aryans in the following migration waves.

Hindu archaeologists said that the Archaeological evidence confirms that the Bengal delta was inhabited by rice-farming communities in the second millennium BCE. People were living in mud housing and producing pottery. Rivers were used for transport while maritime trade boomed in the Bay of Bengal

They also believe that The Iron Age saw coinage, metal weapons, agriculture, and irrigation. Large urban settlements formed in the middle of the first millennium BCE when the Northern Black Polished Ware culture dominated the northern part of the Indian subcontinent. Alexander Cunningham, the founder of the Archaeological Survey of India, identified the archaeological site of Mahasthangarh as the capital of the Pundra Kingdom mentioned in the Rigveda. The Rigveda is an ancient Indian collection of Vedic Sanskrit hymns. It is one of the four sacred recognized religious textbooks of Hinduism, commonly known as the Vedas.

Hindu intellectuals make a historical case that the ancient Bengal is in India's history and Sri Lanka, Siam, Indonesia, Cambodia, Burma, Nepal, Tibet, and China

Reluctant Fathers

Malaya history. Giving reference to the Hindu religious textbook Mahabharata, the Vanga Kingdom had located in Bengal. In the Sri Lankan past, the first king of Sri Lanka was Prince Vijaya, who led a fleet from India to conquer the island of Lanka. Prince Vijaya's ancestral Home was in Bengal.

In the Greek-Roman Era, the Gangaridai Kingdom was believed to be Bengal by historians. At the time of Alexander the Great's invasion of India, the collective might of the Gangaridai and the Nanda Empire (Bihar) prevented the Greek army's advances in India. The archaeological sites

of Wari-Bateshwar and Chandraketugarh are interrelated to the Gangaridai kingdom. In Ptolemy's world map, the emporium of Sounagoura (Sonargaon) is located in Bengal. Roman geographers also noted a large natural harbor in southeastern Bengal, believed to be the present-day Chittagong region.

In short, I have tried my end to enlighten ancient Bengala historical counts to avoid the assumption of being bais as a Muslim. The history books are on the library shelves and the present-day online. There is no reason for me to undermine the thousands of years of Hindu History.

Hinduism

Hinduism is an ancient Indian religion. According to Islamic belief, it is a polytheistic religion contrary to Islamic monotheism. In the view of world historians, it is one of the oldest religions in the world. It also is the world's third-largest religion. Hindu intellectual refer to Hinduism as Sanātana Dharma, which interpreted that its origins lie beyond human history. Hindu scholars view Hinduism as a self-designation of Vaidika dharma, the 'Dharma-related to the Vedas.

My study showed Hinduism is a range of philosophies related to shared religious concepts, recognizable rituals between religions, pilgrimage made to sacred sites, and shared textual resources such as Vedas. That discussed by theologians, philosophers, mythologians, Vedic yajna, yoga, agamic practices, and temple building, prescribes eternal duties, such as honesty, refraining from injuring living beings, and patience, forbearance, self-restraint, virtue, and compassion, among others.

Leading themes in Hinduism beliefs include the four Puruṣārthas, the reasonable goals or aims of human life, namely, Dharma(religion). Artha (prosperity/work), kama (desires/passions), and Moksha (liberation/freedom from the cycle of death and rebirth/salvation), as well as karma (action, intent, and consequences) and saṃsāra (cycle of death and rebirth).

Hindu practices include puja (worship) nearly everything as a form of God and recitations of Shruti and Smriti, Japa, meditation (dhyāna), family-oriented rites of

Reluctant Fathers

passage, annual festivals, and occasional pilgrimages. Along with the practice of various yogas, some Hindus leave their social world and material possessions and engage in lifelong Sannyasa (monasticism) to achieve Moksha.

The Hindu caste system is divided into four main classes - Brahmins, Kshatriyas, Vaishyas, and the Shudras. Many believe that the groups originated from Brahma, the Hindu God of creation. The Brahmin class understood as Hindus a supreme class—brahmin means "Supreme Self." Brahmin is the highest Varna in Vedic Hinduism.

Kshatriya class Hindus understood authority and power. This authority and power are not based on successful leadership, but it inherited generation after generation. Kshatriya is the second Varna within the social hierarchy.

The Vaishyas are a third class in the Hindu Caste System, otherwise known as the ordinary people. According to Yanjur Veda, "Vaisya among men...brutes from the belly. The Hindu scholars defined Vaishyas created from the storehouse of food (stomach) to be the food (or intended to be enjoyed by others).

The Sudras are the fourth class or lowest class of the Hindu Caste System. They usually are artisans and laborers. A large portion of this caste is a product of an upper caste's mating and an Untouchable or a Sudra.

In the cafeteria discussion, Bangladeshi Bengali strongly argue that they were forcefully converted to Islam from Hinduism by the sword. Also, some Hindu claimed that the Sudras were converted to Islam by money and marriage. I can't entirely agree with Bangladeshi Bengali because I am an indigenous Sylheti. I do know that Muslim

Mujaheed did fight against the Hindu Kings for various reasons. But they were not forcing any human beings to convert to Islam. For example, in Sylhet first and only Muslim was Ghazi Burhanuddin. The Sultan of Lakhnauti Shamsuddin Firoz Shah's army defeated the Hindu King Gour Govinda.

This war began when Ghazi Burhanuddin, a Muslim living in Tultikar, sacrificed a cow for his newborn son's *aqiqah* or celebration of birth. King Govinda had the newborn beheaded for what he saw as blasphemy and had Burhanuddin's right hand chopped off. The general's army was aided by an Islamic scholar, Shah Jalal, and his disciples and nephews. Chief minister Mona Rai was killed in the battle, and King Govinda fled with his family.

The Kingdom of Srihatta was then renamed Jalalabad under the **Muslim Sultanate. Sikandar Khan Ghazi**, one of the battle and Firoz's nephew's commanders, then made the first Muslim Amir (ruler) over Sylhet. Sikander ruled for many years under **Shamsuddin Firoz Shah** until his death, when a Hindu traitor shrunk the boat and drowned him to death while riding a boat. Sylheti war is a true story that clarifies that Muslims did not initiate wars or forcefully convert the Hindus.

However, charity work in poor communities may inspire some poor people to revert to Islam that does not necessarily mean that all poor people in Bengal revert to Islam because of Muslim hospitality.

Reluctant Fathers

Buddhism

Folktale that Gautama Buddha came to the Bengal to spread Buddhism. Some Bengali intellectuals believe that one or two disciples came to spread Buddhism in Bengal. However, Buddhism did not apply until the reign of Emperor Asoka, when Buddhism gained political support. According to historians, the Pala Empire that ruled the Indian subcontinent spread Buddhism in Bengal. Bengali Buddhists carry various ideologies in Buddhism than actual Buddah doctrines in modern-day Bangladesh. According to Bangladeshi historians, During the Pala Dynasty, a famous preacher named Atisha was born in Bikrampur and spread Mahayana Buddhism.

1202 War

As history suggested, Muslim traders and preachers gradually migrated to India right after Prophet Muhammed (PBUH) passed away. As Islam took its peak in Bengal and Bihar, the Hindu and Buddhists were frequently annoying Muslims out of their jealousy and envy. Muslims used to always complained to the Muslim rulers in West India for justice. I have given an example from the Sylhet War that cow was a significant issue for Hindus, whereas Muslims use it as food.

Ikhtiyār al-Dīn Muḥammad Bakhtiyār Khaljī decided it is time for action against the petty Kings in Bihar and Bengal. He made a sincere effort to win Bihar in 1200. This victory earned him a political career in the court of Delhi. In the same year, he took his forces into Bengal. As he came upon the city of Nabadwip, it is well-documented that he advanced so rapidly that only 18 horsemen from his army could be keeping up with the battles. He conquered Nabadwip from the old Emperor Lakshmana Sena in 1203.

Subsequently, Khalji captured the capital and the principal city, Gaur. he marched into Bengal. Ikhtiyār al-Dīn Muḥammad Bakhtiyār Khaljī victory one after another against petty kings (Raja) in Bengal. Muslims in Bengal began to believe that Allah is sending angels to help Ikhtiyār al-Dīn Muḥammad Bakhtiyār Khaljī to win over the Musrik Rajas. Those victories over kings help Islam rapidly spread in the region.

Bakhtiyar Khalji's victories are accused of severely damaging the Buddhist establishments at Odantapuri and Vikramashila, which were thought to be fortifications by his army. Historically, everywhere the war has some destruction and damage, so did his. There are high historical account possibilities of war injuries and destruction of the buildings.

In the Chittagong Hills, Buddhist tribes formed most of the population, and their religion appeared to be a mixture of tribal beliefs and Buddhist doctrines. According to the 1981 census, there were approximately 538,000 Buddhists in Bangladesh, representing less than 1 percent of the population.

Reluctant Fathers

Muslim

Muslims are known as monotheistic religious people or one of the Abrahamic religions. Muslims are those who practice Islam. the Messenger of Allah (ﷺ) said, "Islam has built on five [pillars]: testifying that there is nothing worthy of worship except Only One God and that Prophet Muhammad is the Messenger of Allah, establishing (five times) the salah (prayer), paying the zakat (obligatory charity), making the hajj (pilgrimage) to the Makkah, and fasting in the month of Ramadhan." [Bukhari & Muslim]

Islam is not like a Hindu or Buddhist scholar debate on the historical count and archaeological evidence to prove its authenticity. In Islam, historical counts are very different from any other religion in the world. Islamic knowledge derives from two authentic sources, the Quran and authentic hadiths, unlike any other historical studies. For example, Muslims do not believe that human beings randomly evolved from apes. Human beings' lives began with creating two people, a male and a female named Adam and Hawwa (Eve).

Praise be to Allah.

Allaah created Adam with His hand, breathed into him his soul created by Him, and told His angels to prostrate to him. Allaah created Adam from dust, as He says (interpretation of the meaning): "Verily, the likeness of 'Eesa (Jesus) before Allaah is the likeness of Adam. He created him from dust, then (He) said to him: 'Be!' — and he was' ' [Aal 'Imran 3:59]. When Allaah had completed the creation of Adam, He commanded the angels to prostrate to him, so they prostrated, except for Iblees, who was present but he refused and was too arrogant to prostrate to Adam. "(Remember) when your Lord said to the angels: 'Truly, I am going to create man from clay. So when I have fashioned him and breathed into him (his) soul created by Me, then you fall down prostrate to him.' So the angels prostrated themselves, all of them, Except for Iblees (Satan), he was proud and was one of the disbelievers" [Saad 38:71-74 – interpretation of the meaning] Then Allaah told the angels that He was going to place Adam on earth and make generations after generations of his offspring, as He said (interpretation of the meaning): "And (remember) when your Lord said to the angels: 'Verily, I am going to place (mankind) generations after generations on earth'" [al-Baqarah 2:30] Allaah taught Adam all the names: "And He taught Adam all the names (of everything)" [al-Baqarah 2:31 – interpretation of the meaning]

When Iblees refused to prostrate Adam, Allaah expelled him and cursed him: "(Allaah) said: 'Then get out from here; for verily, you are outcast. And verily, My Curse is on you till the Day of Recompense'" [Saad 38:77-78 – interpretation of the meaning] When Iblees knew of his fate, he asked Allaah to give him respite until the Day of Resurrection: "[Iblees (Satan)] said: 'My Lord! Give me then respite till the day the (dead) are resurrected.' (Allaah) said: 'Verily, you are of those allowed respite Till the Day of the time appointed'" [Saad 38:79-81 – interpretation of the meaning] When Allaah granted him that, he declared war on Adam and his descendants, made disobedience attractive to them and tempted them to commit immoral actions: "[Iblees (Satan)] said: 'By Your Might, then I will

Reluctant Fathers

surely, mislead them all, Except Your chosen slaves amongst them (i.e., faithful, obedient, true believers of Islamic Monotheism).'" [Saad 38:82-83 – interpretation of the meaning] Allaah created Adam, and from him, He created his wife, and from their progeny, He created men and women, as He says (interpretation of the meaning): "O mankind! Be dutiful to your Lord, Who created you from a single person (Adam), and from him (Adam) He created his wife [Hawwa (Eve)], and from them both He created many men and women" [al-Nisaa' 4:1]

Then Allaah caused Adam and his wife to dwell in Paradise as a test for them. He commanded them to eat of the fruits of Paradise, but He forbade them to eat from one tree: "And We said: 'O Adam! Dwell you and your wife in the Paradise and eat both of you freely with pleasure and delight, of things therein as wherever you will, but come not near this tree or you both will be of the Zalimoon (wrong-doers)'"

Allaah warned Adam and his wife against the Shaytaan, as He said (interpretation of the meaning): "O Adam! Verily, this is an enemy to you and to your wife. So let him not get you both out of Paradise so that you will be distressed." [Ta-Ha 20:117] Then the Shaytaan whispered to Adam and his wife and tempted them to eat from the forbidden tree. Adam forgot and could not resist the temptation, so he disobeyed his Lord and ate from that tree: "Then Shaytaan (Satan) whispered to him, saying: 'O Adam! Shall I lead you to the Tree of Eternity and to a kingdom that will never waste away?'

Then they both ate of the tree, and so their private parts became manifest to them, and they began to cover themselves with the leaves of the Paradise for their covering. Thus did Adam disobey his Lord, so he went astray." [Ta-Ha 20:120-121 – interpretation of the meaning] Their Lord called to them and said (interpretation of the meaning): "Did I not forbid you that tree and tell you: Verily, Shaytaan (Satan) is an open enemy unto you?" [al-A'raf 7:22]

When they ate from the tree, they regretted what they had done and said: "Our Lord! We have wronged ourselves. If You forgive us not, and bestow not upon us Your Mercy, we shall certainly be of the losers." [al-A'raf 7:23 – interpretation of the meaning]

The sin of Adam stemmed from desire, not from arrogance; hence Allaah guided him to repent, and He accepted that from him: "Then Adam received from his Lord Words. And his Lord pardoned him (accepted his repentance). Verily, He is the One Who forgives (accepts repentance), the Most Merciful." [al-Baqarah 2:37 – interpretation of the meaning]

Repent is the way for Adam and his descendants: whoever sins then regrets sincerely, Allaah will accept his repentance: "And He is Who accepts repentance from His slaves, and forgives sins, and He knows what you do"[al-Shoora 42:25 – interpretation of the meaning] Then Allaah sent Adam and his wife, and Iblees, down to the earth, and He sent down Revelation to them, and He sent the Messengers to them. So whoever believes will enter Paradise and whoever disbelieves will enter Hell: "We said: 'Get down all of you from this place (the Paradise), then whenever there comes to you Guidance from Me, and whoever follows My Guidance, there shall be no fear on them, nor shall they grieve. But those who disbelieve and belie Our Ayaat (proofs, evidence, verses, lessons, signs, revelations, .) — such are the dwellers of the Fire. They shall abide therein forever." [al-Baqarah 2:38-39 – interpretation of the meaning]

When Allaah sent them all down to the earth, the conflict between faith and disbelief, truth and falsehood, good and evil, began, and it will continue until Allaah inherits the world and everyone on it: "(Allaah) said: 'Get down, one of you an enemy to the other [i.e., Adam, Hawwa, (Eve), and Shaytaan (Satan)]. On earth will be a dwelling place for you and an enjoyment for a time.' [al-A'raaf 7:24 – interpretation of the meaning]

Allah is Able to do all things. He created Adam with no father or mother, and He created Hawwa from a father with no mother, and He created 'Eesa from a mother with no father, and He created us from a father and a mother. Allaah created Adam from dust, then He made his descendants from semen of despised water, as He says (interpretation of the meaning): "Who made everything He has created good and He began the creation of man from clay.

Then He made his offspring from semen of despised water (male and female sexual discharge). Then He fashioned him in due proportion and breathed into him the soul (created by Allaah for that person), and He gave you hearing (ears), sight (eyes), and hearts. Little is the thanks you give!" [Al-Sajdah 32:7-9]

How man is created in the womb and the stages he goes through is wondrous. Allaah mentioned this in the aayah (interpretation of the meaning): "And indeed We created man (Adam) out of an extract of clay (water and earth). After that, We made him (the offspring of Adam) as a Nutfah (mixed drops of the male and female sexual discharge and lodged it) in a safe lodging (womb of the woman). Then We made the Nutfah into a clot (a piece of thick coagulated blood), then We made the clot into a little lump of flesh, then We made out of that little lump of flesh bones, then We clothed the bones with flesh, and then We brought it forth as another creation. So Blessed is Allaah, the Best of creation." [al-Mu'minun 23:12-14]

Allaah Alone creates whatever He wills. He knows what is in the wombs, and He decrees provision and lifespans (for His creatures): "To Allah belongs the kingdom of the heavens and the earth. He creates what He wills. He bestows female (offspring) upon whom He wills, and bestows male (offspring) upon whom He wills. He bestows both males and females, and He renders barren whom He wills. Verily, He is the All-Knower and is Able to do all things." [al-Shoora 42:49-50 – interpretation of the meaning]

The Prophet (peace and blessings of Allaah be upon him) said: "Allah has appointed an angel over the womb. He says, 'O Lord, a drop of semen (nutfah); O Lord, a clot ('alaqah); O Lord, a little lump of flesh (mudghah).' Then if Allah wishes (to complete) its creation, the angel asks, (O Lord) male or female, wretched (doomed to Hell) or blessed (destined for Paradise)? How much will his provision be? And what will his lifespan be?' So that is written while (the child) is still in the mother's womb." (Narrated by al-Bukhaari, 318)

"See you not (O men) that Allaah has subjected for you whatsoever is in the heavens and whatsoever is in the earth, and has completed and perfected His Graces upon you, (both) apparent (i.e., Islamic Monotheism, and the lawful pleasures of this world, including health, good looks) and hidden [i.e., one's faith in Allah (of Islamic Monotheism), knowledge, wisdom, guidance for doing righteous deeds, and also the pleasures and delights of the Hereafter in Paradise]? [Luqmaan 31:20 – interpretation of the meaning]

Allaah has distinguished and an honored man with reason by which he knows his Lord, Creator, and Provider, and by which he knows what is right and evil, what will benefit him and what will harm him, what is halaal and what is haraam. Allaah did not create man and leave him alone with no path to follow. Instead, Allaah revealed the Books and sent Messengers to guide humanity to the Straight Path.

Allaah created people with a natural inclination towards monotheism (Tawhid – belief in the Oneness of Allah). Every time they deviated from that, Allaah sent a Prophet to bring them back to the Straight Path. The first of the Prophets was Adam, and the last was Muhammad (peace and blessings of Allaah be upon him):

Mankind was one community, and Allaah sent Prophets with glad tidings and warnings. With them, He sent down the Scripture in truth to judge between people in matters wherein they differed [al-Baqarah 2:213 – interpretation of the meaning] All the Messengers called people to the same fact, which is the worship of Allah alone and to reject all false gods besides Him: "And verily, We have sent among every Ummah (community, nation) a Messenger (proclaiming): "Worship Allah (Alone), and avoid (or keep away from) Taaghoot (all false deities, i.e., do not worship Taaghoot besides Allaah)." [al-Nahl 16:36 – interpretation of the meaning]

The religion with which Allaah sent the Prophets and Messengers was the same, i.e., Islam: "Truly, the religion with Allaah is Islam." [Aal 'Imraan 3:19 –

interpretation of the meaning] The last of the heavenly Books which Allaah revealed was the Qur'an, confirming the Books which came before it, and as a guide to all of mankind:

The last of the Prophets and Messengers whom Allaah sent was Muhammad (peace and blessings of Allaah be upon him): "Muhammad is not the father of any of your men, but he is the Messenger of Allaah and the last (end) of the Prophets." [al-Ahzaab 33:40 – interpretation of the meaning] Allaah sent Muhammad (peace and blessings of Allaah be upon him) to all of mankind: "Say (O Muhammad): 'O mankind! Verily, I am sent to you all as the Messenger of Allah'" [al-A'raf 7:158 – interpretation of the meaning] [Aal 'Imran 3:85 – interpretation of the meaning]

The religion which was brought by Muhammad (peace and blessings of Allaah be upon him) confirms the message conveyed by the Prophets before him, in its basic principles and advocation of noble characteristics, as Allaah says (interpretation of the meaning): "He (Allaah) has ordained for you of religion (Islamic Monotheism) what He ordained for Nooh (Noah), and that which We have revealed to you (O Muhammad), and that which We ordained for Ibraaheem (Abraham), Moosa (Moses) and 'Eesa (Jesus) saying you should establish the religion (i.e., to do what it orders you to do practically) and make no divisions] therein (religion, i.e., various sects in religion). [al-Shoora 42:13]

As many of my non-Muslims college friends in the late 95s, Hindu, Christian, Jews, Shia, speculated that I am hiding something about Muslim belief from them to make myself more fitting with them. The above verses of the Quran can be verified or searched online. I have no reason

Reluctant Fathers

to lie or fabricated the knowledge from any of the children of Adam.

So Jesus said to the Jews who had believed him, "If you abide in my word, you are truly my disciples, [32] and you will know the truth, and the truth will set you free." John 8:32

The Messenger of Allaah (peace and blessings of Allaah be upon him) said, "Those who came before you of the people of the Book split into seventy-two sects, and this ummah will split into seventy-three sects. seventy-two in Hell and one in Paradise and that is the jama'ah (main body of Muslims)."

As we know, Prophet Muhammed (peace and blessings of Allaah be upon him) predicted Muslim will be divided into seventy-three sects. It is better to adhere to the Quran and authentic Hadith to avoid religious tension among Muslims and non-Muslim alike.

Reluctant Fathers

Muslim Sultanate

Muslim Sultanate began in Bengal with **Bakhtiar Khilji**'s victory of Gauda between 1202 and 1204 during Muhammad of Ghor's reign. After the Muslim victory, Sunni Muslims became the dominant power in Bengal. After the assassination of Bakhtiar Khalji by the traitor Ali Mardan in 1206, Bengal felt under various Maliks (Landowners) except for a brief interruption by traitor Ali Mardan himself. Until Delhi Sultan **Iltutmish** sent forces under his son's leadership to restore the central governmental authority over Bengal, General Nasir-ud-din Mahmud successfully brought Bengal under the Delhi governmental control. Iltutmish declared Bengal as a province of Delhi in 1225. The Delhi government established a systematic governing capacity in Bengal by appointing **Nawab** (governors).

However, Delhi could not successfully administer Bengal because of Bengal and Delhi distance and challenging communications. Disloyal governors rebelled against the Delhi government and declared Independence, including my great-great-grandfather, and he was recognized as Mirasdar (Lord). Delhi's Government militarily taught a lesson to the rebellious governors but recognized local Mirasdari. However, there were various self-declared rulers among the rebels, including Yuzbak Shah (1257), Tughral Khan (1271–1282), and **Shamsuddin Firoz Shah** (1301–1322). The latter achieved the **Jihad of Sylhet** and established a robust administration in eastern and south-western Bengal. In 1325, the Delhi Sultan **Ghiyath al-Din Tughluq** reorganized the province into three administrative regions, with **Sonargaon** ruling

Reluctant Fathers

eastern Bengal; Gauda ruling northern Bengal; Satgaon ruling southern Bengal.

Also, the partition of Bengal did not work as was thought. In 1338, the three administrative regions had self-declared Sultans, including Fakhruddin Mubarak Shah in Sonargaon, Alauddin Ali Shah in Gauda Shamsuddin Ilyas Shah in Satgaon. Fakhruddin declared Jihad against Chittagong Buddiest petty tribal rulers in 1340 because of overwhelming complaints against petty tribal chieftains for systematically harassing Muslims in Chittagong. Ikhtiyaruddin Ghazi Shah, son of Fakruddin victory in 1349, earned him the title Ghazi from Delhi government and from the Muslims messes, the highest honorable title for living Mujahed. Shamsuddin Ilyas Shah (or just Ilyas Shah) defeated Alauddin Ali Shah and secured control of Gauda. He then defeated Ikhtiyaruddin of Sonargaon. By 1352, Ilyas Shah emerged victorious among the Bengali triad.

As we briefly scrutinized the history of Bengal, we have learned that the Hindu Upper Caste and Buddhists tribal chieftain systematically harassed Muslims in Bengal. The fundamental problems were between Muslims and Hindu cow scarifying, handshaking, defecting on the paddy field. Defecting on the paddy field was a serious issue because Muslims call it "Nizasa." The early Muslims in Bengal always had Hindu and Buddist problems based on the cultural and social aspects.

The early Muslims in Bengal lived in Hindu communities; their grandfather or great-grandfather migrated to Bengal for trade or preaching Islam. They bought lands from Hindu petty Kings and settling within the community. The new influx of Muslims came to fight against petty Hindu Kings and declared themselves as Kings. In contrast, early Muslims lived within Hindu and Buddist communities, which was the most significant psychological problem in Bengal for the last thousand years. Early Muslims wanted to live with Hindu, Buddist, and Christan in peace and harmony. The newcomer wanted to exile all the non-Muslim from Bengal.

Shia Rule

Shia rule in Bengal was one of the confusing times in Bengal for Muslims. The Persians were migrating to Bengal after the Muslim victory in Bengal in 1202. The Persian language penetrated in Bengali Muslim language that changed formerly used Arabic words such as sawm to Roza, Salah to Namaz. Many other Arabic words were replaced by Farsi. The Persians were welcomed in the Muslim Sultanate in Bengal for two specific reasons. No. 1, their thousands of years old military experience under the Persian empire to use it in the military training in Bengal. No. 2, for their skin color. As indigenous Bengali skin color was very dark and Persian skin color was a little lighter. These are two specific reasons Persians were allowed to settle in Muslim Bengal.

As history self-evident, Muslims divided into two groups right after Khalifa Umer's (Radeyallāhu 'Anhu) assassination. In 644, Omar (Radeyallāhu 'Anhu) was assassinated by a Persian named Abu Lulu by later accounts. His motivation for the assassination was not clear to this day—Islamic historians and Islamic scholars of Aqidah much on dispute this matter. One widespread rationalization was that it was done in response to the Muslim victory over Persian Empire. The other is a conspiracy theory that few Muslims (Sunni) believe Shi'ism originated from Persia as a Jews conspiracy because the

Reluctant Fathers

theological father of Shi'ism is 'Abdullah ibn Saba' al-Ḥimyarī.

However, Islamic scholars of Aqeedah believe Shia originated from a convert Jews Rabbi 'Abdullah ibn Saba' al-Ḥimyarī. The political science scholars believe that Shiism began as a political faction rather than a religious sect as they use the evidence of Umer's (Radeyallāhu 'Anhu) assassination.

Some Sunni believe that the Persians wanted to spread Shiaism in Bengal; that's why they are changing the Islamic language (mix with Arabic and local languages) to Farsi language, whereas Bengal was a hardcore Sunni stronghold. However, the Persians did not come to Bengal for religious preaching or trades' purposes. The Arabs were mainly welcomed as Islamic religious preachers and traders. The Arabs were well-known for their honesty in business transactions and Islamic knowledge. There is no evidence related to Persian dominance in the field of religious education in Bengal. Of course, Persian works of literature were widespread in Bengal stories and poems.

The difference between Shia and Sunni, I did not know before. One day, I prayed Maghrib in a Shia Masjid in Jamaica, Queens, NY. My brother told me that it's a Shia Masjid. I asked him what's the difference between Shia and Sunni. He said, "I don't know, but they pray differently than us. I said I noticed that.

I have thoroughly studied under some prestigious Islamic scholars to understand Shia and Muslims' (Sunnah) differences. I found we Muslims heavily differed with Shia in the matter of Aqidah (creed). the number one authentic scholar in Islam said about Shia by referring to an authentic Hadith The Messenger of Allah (ﷺ) said, "He who innovates something in this matter of ours (i.e., Islam) that is not of it will have it rejected (by Allah)." [Bukhari & Muslim]

Reluctant Fathers

Historians argued that Persian resident Piruz Nahavandi (Abu Lulu) complained to Omar (Radeyallāhu 'Anhu) about the high tax charged by his local ruler Mughirah. Omar (Radeyallāhu 'Anhu) wrote to Mughirah regarding the high tax; Mughirah's response was satisfied, but Omar (Radeyallāhu 'Anhu) told Abu Lulu the tax was reasonable, based on his income. Omar (Radeyallāhu 'Anhu) asked Abu Lulu: "I heard that you make windmills; make one for me as well." In a sullen mood, Piruz said, "Verily, I will make such a mill for you that the whole world would remember it."

It was Piruz who was assigned the mission of assassinating Omar (Radeyallāhu 'Anhu). According to the hearsay story, before the Fajr prayers (the morning prayers before the dawn), Piruz would enter Al-Masjid al-Nabawi, the central Masjid of Caliphate where Omar (Radeyallāhu 'Anhu) led the prayers and would attack Omar (Radeyallāhu 'Anhu) during the prayers, and then flee or mix with the congregation at the mosque.

On October 31, 644, Piruz attacked Omar (Radeyallāhu 'Anhu) while leading in the Masjid morning prayers. Piruz stabbed him six times in the belly, and on the navel, it was a severe injury. Omar (Radeyallāhu 'Anhu) was bleeding while people were running to catch Piruz. Before fleeing Medin. in his efforts to escape, he ended up committing suicide. He injured approximately nine of the people Masjid who later died, before slashing himself with his blade to commit suicide—left his motive in suspense.

Some Islamic scholars hold the view that Omar (Radeyallāhu 'Anhu) always wanted to be a myrtle after reverting to Islam because he became a Khalifa. He can not participate on the battlefield, but Allah accepted him as a myrtle. It is essential to mention that if some got killed, that person is considered a myrtle in Islam.

Reluctant Fathers

In Bengal, Sarfarāz Khān was widely accused of spreading Shiism in Bengal; that is why Sunni Muslims were boycotting him. Sunni upper middle class (Mirasdar/Malik) tradition sent one of their sons to join the military to defend the Muslim states. But, from Sarfarāz Khān, they stop sending their children. That's why Sarfarāz Khān used to heavily depend on the Hindu Kshatriya caste and make them Zamindars.

East India Company Rules

East Indian Company rule in India is highly controversial between Indian freedom fighters, Hindu nationalists, Muslims in Bengal, and ordinary Indians. Most ordinary Indians appreciate the Company rule in Bengal and India. According to my college cafeterias' political discussion with the regular Indian students, they defend Company, and British governments rule in India. They argued that without East India Company rule in Bengal, India would have remained a thousands of years old backward caste system. And technologically, bureaucratically, the judicial system, post office system, telegram office, and railroads developments India would be one of the undeveloped African countries.

Most Indians often misunderstand East India Company rules as British Rule. In reality, East India Company was a mega-corporation founded in London in 1600. Understanding India's internal ongoing conflict, The Company created a policy to support small, petty kings with money and military logistics with a treaty. Fundamentally, it was doing unconventional banking and unregulated interstate tradings.

Historically, the East India Company first came to India in 1612. King James (I) sent Sir Thomas Roe to visit

Reluctant Fathers

the Mughal Emperor Nur-ud-din Salim Jahangir (r. 1605–1627) to create a trade treaty that would give the Company exclusive rights to reside and build the businesses in Surat and other areas.

In return, the Company offered to provide the Emperor with goods and rarities from the European market. King James (I) expectation was satisfied, Emperor Jahangir sent a letter to King James through Sir Thomas Roe

"Upon which assurance of your royal love I have given my general command to all the kingdoms and ports of my dominions to receive all the merchants of the English nation as the subjects of my friend; that in what place soever they choose to live, they may have free liberty without any restraint; and at what port soever they shall arrive, that neither Portugal nor any other shall dare to molest their quiet; and in what city soever they shall have residence, I have commanded all my governors and captains to give them freedom answerable to their own desires; to sell, buy, and to transport into their country at their pleasure. For confirmation of our love and friendship, I desire your Majesty to command your merchants to bring in their ships of all sorts of rarities and rich goods fit for my palace; and that you be pleased to send me your royal letters by every opportunity, that I may rejoice in your health and prosperous affairs; that our friendship may be interchanged and eternal".

The reason Emperor Nur-ud-din Salim Jahangir was generous with Thomas Roe because of the Quranic verse "Ahl al-kitābto (people of the Book). The Ahl al-kitāb refer to Jews, Christians, and Sabians. According to Islam, people of the books are monotheistic religious people known as Abrahamic religion and Hindus known as Musrik (Polytheistic religion).

However, East India Company was gradually increasing its influence on the port cities in the Indian subcontinent. So did Bengal.

The Battle of Plassey

The battle of Plassey is widely well-known in the Indian subcontinent and by the British. There are hundreds of books written, and movies were made about this war. The story of the Plassey is not a straightforward political situation to explain in brief. I would only touch the core of it. As East India Company realized, the central Government of Delhi is in a deep internal political crisis. The Company created a strategy to use the petty kings against each other by promising to provide military training, financial assistance with a low-interest rate, and a reasonable trade deal.

Lord Clive was a sharp brain brilliant. He recognized that Indians have a nervous caste system and Muslims are an insignificant minority but a ruling class in India. Also, Muslims are divided into two groups, Shia and Sunni. The Sunni will not support the Shia government, And again, Mirza Muhammad Siraj-ud-Daulah does not have a good relationship with the Central Government. That gave him a sense of fearlessly creating a conspiracy to buy out Siraj-ud-Daulah generals. He was successful in this conspiracy. Without shedding blood, he easily won the war.

Lord Clive calculated the entire geopolitical crisis pretty well. His political calculation was a turning point in subcontinent history and opened the way to eventual British rule. His victory in the Plassey war was a most significant achievement for the British Government for hundreds of years.

Reluctant Fathers

Historically, After Siraj-ud-Daulah's success of Calcutta, the East India Company sent new troops from Madras to retake the fort and take revenge on the attack. To retreat, Siraj-ud-Daulah met the British at Plassey. He built military camps approximately twenty-five miles away from Murshidabad.

On June 23, 1757, Siraj-ud-Daulah called on Mir Jafar because he was dismayed by the sudden death of Mir Mardan, who was the trustworthy general of Siraj in battles. The Nawab asked for advice from Mir Jafar. Mir Jafar advised Nawab to retreat for that day. The Nawab made a strategic mistake on the battlefield in giving the order to stop the fight. Following his command, the soldiers of the Nawab were returning to their camps. In the war strategy, you never stop a fight in the middle of the war without a cease-fire agreement declaration by both parties.

At the same time, Robert Clive attacked the Nawab soldiers with his army on the battlefield. He took full advantage of the unilateral cease-fire. In a situation like this, any general will take full advantage of the self-declared cease-fire. It indicates that the enemies are weakened; it is time for a decisive victory.

At a decisive attack, the army of Nawab was heading to the camps for rest because of the Nawab order, and it was very difficult to reorder for the counter-attack. So all fled away from the battlefield. This defeat was well-planned by Lord Clive, Jagat Seth, Mir Jafar, Krishna Chandra, Omichund. Before the war began, Lord Clive, Jagat Seth, Mir Jafar, Krishna Chandra, Omichund had a roundtable meeting to orchestrate a defeat in the Plassey against Nawab.

Betrayal of Mir Jafar in Plassey, Nawab, lost the war and had to flee to avoid an arrest. He went first to

Reluctant Fathers

Murshidabad, specifically to Hirajheel, his palace at Mansurganj. He ordered his senior commanders to bring their troops for his safety, but as he was defeated at Plassey, they refused to obey his order and supported him to defend the palace. Some advised him to surrender himself up to the Company. Nawab realized it is well planned, and all of them are treacherous. A few loyal commanders recommend that he encourage the army with greater rewards, which he seemed to approve. But, it was too late. The entire chain of command collapsed.

On July 2, 1757, Siraj-ud-Daulah was executed by Muhammad Ali Beg under Mir Miran's orders, son of Mir Jafar in Namak Haram Deorhi, and agreement between Mir Jafar and the British East India Company to kill Siraj-ud-Daulah. It was an end to Independent so-called Muslim Bengal.

Hindu Zamindars

The Plassey defeat was a total shock for Sunni Muslims in East Bengal. Muslims were confident that Nawab would win the war easily because he had generous support from Hindus or Delhi would come to help him. However, the defeat was not a piece of good news for Muslims as a whole in India. The Company had become a de facto ruler in line with Mir Jafar's rule.

Despite this, the East India Company created the Hindu Zamindari system by using force, taking the land from Muslim Malik/Mirasdar. They leased those land for ninety-nine years. A low-interest loan to build houses to operate the Zamindari The Company was auctioning the Zamindari to only two Hindu upper Kshatriya and Brahmin castes. Historically, the Shia rulers established the

Reluctant Fathers

Zamindari system. Zamin is a Farsi word for land, and dar is an Arabic word for Home Zamindar means a Landlord. As the East India Company originated from Europe, they knew how feudalism works. They used that feudalism very wisely in India.

The rise of Hindu Zamindars during the East India Company rule created a vicious cycle of discriminatory social culture in Bengal. The Hindu Zamindars deliberately abused poor Muslims in Bengal because they profoundly believe that the Sudras caste converted to Islam to gain social status. According to Hinduism, the Sudras were the lowest caste.

As some of my Hindu friends argued that we Muslims also have a caste system. Actually, in the Muslim community, it is not a caste system. It is more like a social hierarchy system. This system does not encourage or discourage Islam. In the Quran, Allah said,

" Say: "O Allah! Possessor of the power, You give power to whom You will, and You take power from whom You will, and You endue with honor whom You will, and You humiliate whom You will. In Your Hand is good. Verily, You are able to do all things.)" 3:26.

As we believe the honor comes from Allah, that's why most khandani Muslims are humble toward Allah. Born in a Muslim khandani family is not an easy thing, as some people assumed. To be humble requires controlling the ego, arrogance, pride. Tolerating low-class people's behavior is not easy. Respecting the khandani people is a Sunnah (tradition), not obligatory as Hinduism's core religious belief.

Some Malik compromised with the Company to receive the Zamindari title to protect their assets from East

Reluctant Fathers

India Company seizures, but my great grandfather never compromised. Our Mirasdari survived as an independent mirasdar until the East Pakistan government dissolved it in 1950 under the land reform act.

The Zamindari system did not do any benefit to the Muslims or Hinduism in Bengal. It only benefited the East India Company and British Government. Muslims in Bengal were becoming more insufficient and lower due to high taxes and high-interest rates.

British Rule

The British Rules, known as British Raj, indicate British rule on the Indian subcontinent between 1858 and 1947. It lasted nearly a hundred years when the British provinces of the Indian subcontinent were partitioned into two countries: India and Pakistan, allowing the British princely states to choose between these new countries.

The British Raj was under the British Crown rulers as petty kings in the Indian subcontinent from 1858- 1947 who gave allegiance to the British Crown instead of Delhi. The British Government was responsible for defense, foreign policy, and economy. A Royal Crown judicial system was introduced to ensure justice under the British Empire decreed. British Raj was under the British Crown Jurisdiction; that's why it was also called British India.

This system of governance was formed on June 28, 1858, when, after the **Indian Rebellion of 1857,** the **British East India Company** transferred power to the British Crown **Queen Victoria** (who, in 1876, was proclaimed **Empress of India**).

Reluctant Fathers

The capital of the British Raj was in Calcutta between 1858-1911. The British Government decided to relocate the capital to Delhi because of Muslim and Hindu's continual social unrest in Bengal.

On August 15, 1947, British Raj was permanently dissolved by creating two countries India and Pakistan. They were leaving millions of people to die in the Hindu Muslim riot and creating an unimaginable refugee crisis that the world ever experienced. Law and order were a collapse in the new Pakistan. The end of British rule was not joyous for millions, and it created a wound that no one can heal.

Lord Curzon

Lord Curzon played critical rules for Muslims in Bengal. After Hindu Zamindari's sharp rise, between Hindu and Muslim tension was rising, and village to village quarrel intensified. It has become the daily duty for Mirasdar or Malik to hear poor Muslims complain about Hindu Raja or Zamindar harassment, torture, and systematic discriminatory abuses based on religious affiliation such as lynching.

When Lord Curzon was appointed as Viceroy and Governor-General of India, he expressed his desire to meet with Muslims Nawab, Mirasdar, and Malik. Muslims met with Lord Curzon, including my great grandfather Muhammed Hasim Khalisdar; they expressed their concern that Hindu Zamindars systematically humiliate poor Muslims. Therefore they want an Independent Muslim country. Lord Curzon denied the creation of an independent nation, but he will work on the partition of Bengal if they

Reluctant Fathers

promise him that they will come to a political process and end the violence. They agreed with Lord Curzon's proposal.

Partition of Bengal

Bengal's partition was not a new idea for Muslims; Muslims united Bengal by toppling down small, petty kings from small towns and villages since 1200AD. In 1325, Bengal was partitioned by the Muslim Sultanate in Delhi. As Muslims knew the history of the partition of Bengal, that's why they did not object to the breakup of Bengal; instead, they agreed with Lord Curzon on the proposal to partition Bengal.

On July 19, 1905, Lord Curzon announced that Bengal would be divided into East Bengal and West Bengal. Hearing that Bangladeshi Bengali heart and mind highly admired the son of an East Bengal Zamindar family, Rabindranath Tagore, wrote a song "Amar Sonar Bangla." It is essential to mention that the Rabindranath Tagore family used to control one-third of East Bengal Zamindari. And their residential palace was in Calcutta, West Bengal; it was heartbroken for his family when they learned that East Bengal would be on Muslims' hand.

Nearly thirty percent of East Bengali was Rabindranath Tagore, the family's proza. They were the ones who used to complain against the Tagore family's systematic social humiliation to Muslims Mirasdar, Nawab, or Malik. Today their descendants identified them as Bengali can not be a Bengali until singing this song, "Amar Sonar Bangla." The history is very ironic.

The main reason for the partition of Bengal was Hindu Zamindars socially discriminating Muslim Krishak (farmers) Praja (technically means slaves in Hindu

Scripture), preventing them from getting British Governmental job. The British Governmental job was created in line with the Hindu caste system. 1st, 2nd, 3rd, and 4th class job. The first class job was allocated for British, Hindu Kshatriya, Brahmin caste, and Muslim upper class such as Mirasdar, Malik, or Nawab. The Kshatriya and few Muslims dominated the second-class job. The third class job was also dominated by Hindu Vaishyas caste, a few Muslims, but supervisory or head of the third class job positions were designated to the British. The Hindu Sudras caste dominated the fourth class job, but the fourth class job's supervisory or head was a Muslim, but rarely a few Hindu because Hindu other three castes do not like the fourth class job.

Nevertheless, the authorities of the British Raj implemented a territorial reorganization of the Bengal Presidency. The act was executed on October 16, 1905. As lord Curzon promised to Muslims, he kept his promise.

On December 30, 1906, Muslim League was formed. My grandfather, Muhammed Massim Khalisdar, delegated from the State of Assam to support the Muslim League's formation as a political party within compliance with British Legal Framarworks to serve the Muslims' interest in India. Muslims in Bengal and Assam kept their promise as Lord Curzon did.

From 1772 to 1858, all Zamindari certifications known as Deed or Dalil were issued to Hindus only by the East India Company that created a substantial number of Hindu rich people in Bengal within a hundred years. They had gained a high political and economic capacity to influence the British decision-making bodies in India. They lobbied with British Lawmakers in London to Reunite Bengal. Their worst fear was that Muslims would return to the Malik system, which means land ownership. And Hindu

Reluctant Fathers

Zamindars only leased from East India Company that made significant psychological warfare.

The Malik system is in accordance with Islamic Law, known as Sharia. It means a person is a landowner by inheriting or buying or receiving land as a gift, and if a land was unused for 3-5 years, a homeless Muslim could take the land for his shelter. Muslims pay Zakat, Nisab, and sometimes taxes to the Muslim Government to run the state efficiently. That made them nervous in contrast to the British land ownership law.

After the Hindu Influencer's strongly lobbied in London, Lord Hardinge decided to reunite Bengal. It was an appeasement to Hindu Zamindars and Business owners sentiment. Hindus scared the British establishment in London that Muslims will implement Sharia by replacing Crown rules. They accused Muslims of looting, and cow meats are thrown at the Hindu houses where Hindus revered Cow as a Sacred Animal. Hindu women are taken as Khadima. The British Indian economy will collapse if the Islamic Law is implemented in Bengal.

According to the British royal decree, King George announced in December 1911 that Eastern Bengal would be assimilated into the Bengal Presidency, bypassing the British Parliamentary hearing on the reunification of Bengal on the ground urgently required to defuse the violence in Bengal. That was a new turning point for Muslim politics in Bengal. Muslims in Bengal understood it as a breach of trust and decided to walk toward creating a Muslim country.

Reluctant Fathers

Bengali Nationalism

On 14 April 2004, the BBC the opinion poll with the title Greatest Bengali, the poll named Sheikh Mujibur Rahman as the greatest Bengali of all times. . I deeply thought why Sheikh Mujibur Rahman is the greatest of Bengali all times. I realized that by using him 1969-71, Bengali liberated themselves from Muslimization during the Pakistan period in Bengal.

Historically, the Bengali Nationalist movement was created by The Tagore family known as Bengali Renaissance. Rabindranath Tagore, Dwarkanath Tagore, who were leaders of this period, had the vision to make educational reform in Bengali language and make the official language as Bengali. The contribution to the Bengal Renaissance was not the only Tagore family. Several other families members, such as Gaganendranath, Jyotirindranath, Abanindranath, Jyotirindranath Tagore, Asit Kumar Haldar, and Jnanadanandini Devi, had been associated with the movement

After the Mutiny of 1857, the British Government favored the academically introducing regional languages in educational institutions that significantly outweighed Bengali literature. While Ram Mohan Roy and Iswar Chandra Vidyasagar were the pioneers, others like Bankim Chandra Chatterjee, Pramatha Chaudhuri, Upendrakishore Ray Chowdhury, Dwarkanath Ganguly broadened it and built a strong intellectual foundation. In contrast, Mujib started his political career in the late 40s as a Muslim League street picketer and Huseyn Shaheed Suhrawardy's office tea-boy.

The Tagore family was one of the biggest Hindu Zamindars in East Bengal. The Tagore family influence was directly connected with King George; that's why they could do a robust

Reluctant Fathers

Bengali movement. As Bangladeshi Bengali highly admired Sheik Mujibur Rahman, the savers of Bengali, they crowned him the all-time greatest Bengali. Historically or politically, he had no contribution to the Bengali Movement at all.

On March 21, 1948, Governor-General of Pakistan Mohammad Ali Jinnah addressed a large crowd at the Dhaka RaceCourse Field. He sounded like a dictator in his speech. He called out the enemies and conspirators against Pakistan instead of asking for unity for the new Pakistan. That showed Jinnah's lack of intelligence and wisdom, or he deliberately disregarded United Pakistan. Jinnah made it clear that "Urdu and Urdu alone" would be Pakistan's state's language. In contrast, Bengalis are the majority in new Pakistan.

The linguistical tension between Urdu or Bengal reignited by Governor-general Khawaja Nazimuddin (it is significant to mention that my father was pro-Urdu and Muslim League Khawaja Naziuddin group) arrogantly defended the "Urdu-only" policy in a speech on 27 January 1952.

On 31 January, 1952, the Shorbodolio Kendrio Rashtrabhasha Kormi Porishod (All-Party Central Language Action Committee) was formed at the Bar Library Hall meeting University Dhaka, chaired by Maulana Bhashani. He proposed writing the Bengali language in Arabic script in the meeting. The committee opposed the idea at the meeting.

The action committee called for an all-out protest on 21 February to demand Bengali as Pakistan's official language. Including strikes and rallies in the entire East Bengal. To prevent the demonstration, Chief Minister Nurul Amin imposed Section 144 in Dhaka, thereby banning any gathering.

Reluctant Fathers

Those who were not born in a traditional Muslim family would make it challenging for them to understand why most Muslim Leaguers wanted Urdu as an official language. Even the number one outspoken political leader Maulana Bhashani wanted to use Arabic script instead of Bengali. Let me give you a brief historical problem in Bengal.

Muslims migrated to Bengal for trading and preaching Islam from Khaleej, Yemen, and later Turk and Persians. When Muslims were migrating from Khaleej and Yemen that time there was no unified Bengal, it was filled with small, petty kings known as Raja. In 1202, Ikhtiyār al-Dīn Muḥammad Bakhtiyār Khaljī unified the Bengal and Established Muslim Sultanate.

Those Rajas used to have official Mandir, and every Mandir used to have a preacher that preachers used to recite the mantra. The mantra was in the Sanskrit Language. And every local raja used to have their local language. Khaleeji and Yemani both used to speak Arabic. When someone reverted to Islam, they taught them Arabic and explained Arabic words with the broken local language. That's how a new Muslim language was born in Bengal.

In the fourteen century, the Persians migrated to Bengal. The Farsi language gradually penetrated Bengali Muslim language that changed formerly used Arabic words such as sawm to Roza, Salah to Namaz, many other Arabic words., and Parsi literature stories and poems were spreading. The Sunni establishment started getting angry. The fear of spreading Shiism in Bengal. It needs to be noted, Khaleeji and Yemani Muslims were Sunni, and Parisians were mixing with Sunni, Shia, and Zoroastrianism

Reluctant Fathers

Muslim in Bengal defined Farsi as a Shia Language, and Bengali is a Hindu Language than what left? They have invented a new language name Urdu mix with Arabic and local Indian Language. That's why after the creation of Pakistan, they kept pushing for Urdu as the official language and undermining most people's wishes.

The entire language movement history is misunderstood and misinterpreted by almost everyone. Of course, Hindu intellectually worked tirelessly to make the Bengali language an internationally recognized language. That touched their ego and intensified their envy of the orchestrated Bengali language movement.

Almost everyone believes, Bengali language movement ended for United Pakistan. I disagree with this argument. As a grandson of a Muslim League founding member and son of a late Muslim League leader, I am confident that Jinnah was the leading cause of Pakistan's internal and external problem. Jinnah was a simple opportunist and a puppet. Not a politician.

Muslim League

I heard from my Boro Ma (culturally, we call Boro Ma to a woman who comes to the family as the first wife for uncles or father's Cousins) in bedtime story that my grandfather took a horse to go to Dhaka to take part in the Muslim League meeting. Dhaka Nawab sent risalah (Officially invitation) to my great grandfather Muhammed Hasim Khalisdar, but he refused to go to Dhaka due to his health concern. Instead, in winter, my grandfather Muhammed Masim Khalisdar went as one of the Assam state delegates.

Reluctant Fathers

My grandfather went to the meeting not because he agreed with creating a political party. He went to the summit only because my great grandfather promised Lord Curzon that he would be part of a political process if he partitioned the Bengal. Prophet (peace and blessings of Allaah be upon him) said: "There are four (characteristics), whoever has them is a hypocrite, and whoever has one of the four has a characteristic of hypocrisy unless he gives it up: when he speaks, he lies; when he makes a promise he breaks it; what he makes a pledge he betrays it; and when he disputes he resorts to foul language." Narrated by al-Bukhaari, 2327; Muslim, 58.

On December 30, 1906, Muslim League was formed on record. The objective was to educate Muslims in mathematics, English, Science, and Quran. To integrate Muslims with the British Government. To encourage Muslims to take British Governmental jobs because most Muslims used to avoid British. They used to curse them "Bania." or "Guerrilla attacks them." It was the first time in Muslim history that Muslims politically organized to increased political advancement in Bengal and Assam. And Muslim League also laid out a foundation working toward uniting Muslims in India.

Mullah issued a Fatawi that those who learn English are Kafir.Muslim League played down on this Fatawa And advice to all Muslim Leaguer to teach their children to learn English to compete with Hindus.

During the lunch break, some Muslim Leaguers asked Dhaka Nawab to build a University in Dhaka. The Nawab laughed and said, "we just have a new province and just formed a new party. Can we not wait for a few more years". And everyone laughed at the hall.

However, Muslim League was stuck inside of Muslim bourgeois class. It was failing to reach out to

Reluctant Fathers

ordinary Muslims. Muslim League decided to hire Maulana Bhashani, internationally known as Red Maulana, to work with the poor Muslim to support the Muslim League agenda. He was highly flip-flopped. It was tough to trust him. The inner circle of Muslim Leaguer wanted to use him as a counter to the Gandhi movement. Maulana Bhashani did bring Muslim League into the limelight. He made Muslim League a hundred years ahead of the time in Assam and Bengal.

On 16 August 1946, Muslim League declared a day of a nationwide protest leading by Jinnah. It led to large-scale violence between Muslims and Hindus in Calcutta in the Bengal province of British India. This incident has a fascinating background. Bangladeshi Bengali Father Sheikh Mujibur Rahman narrated this story to East Bengal Muslim League Leaders after creating Awami Muslim League that "we three made Pakistan, "Jinnah, Huseyn Shaheed Suhrawardy and I." "so don't question our patriotism."

According to the Mujib claim, Jinnah telegrammed Huseyn Shaheed Suhrawardy, Chief Minister of Bengal, that "There is a piece of information that British Government wants to change the Governor-General. Under the new administration, it would be harder to make a case for Pakistan". Chief Minister of Bengal, Huseyn Shaheed Suhrawardy, responded to the Jinnah telegramme under British Governmental confidentiality rules, "all the options are on the table except partition of Bengal." That was a signal for the Calcutta riot.

After the telegraph, Huseyn Shaheed Suhrawardy asked Mujib in his office, "Khoka, can you take care of the Calcutta?" Mujib said, "Jee Sir." It needed to be noted, Mujib was very close to Huseyn Shaheed Suhrawardy. In the 1946 election, Mujib was Huseyn Shaheed Suhrawardy,

Reluctant Fathers

right-hand man. The Bengal Provincial Muslim League won the 1946 general election. Compared to smaller assembly seats in other Muslim majority provinces in India, the League received its largest Assembly seats in Bengal. The result was interpreted as a referendum for Pakistan. How did Mujib come close to Huseyn Shaheed Suhrawardy? That's a mystery. No one knows for a fact.

During the riot, Shen came to my father's house in Howrah, India. He was my father's college friend. He told my father to get to the Jeep, quickly "I will drop you close to Benapole." My dad asked him, "why"? He said, "butcher of Calcutta, the Khoka gang mercilessly killing Hindu and looting Hindo stores. In retaliation, Hindu mobs are killing Muslims and looting Muslim property. I heard you are a target because you were a Muslim Student activist in the college. They are coming after you. You have two choices. Stay and die or go with me to save your life. I can't wait that long; they will kill me, too."

My father got into Shen Jeep with a few of his other friends. My dad's eyes were filled with tears because of leaving the house. The house was built by my great-great-grandfather hundred years ago. Today, he has to leave it in the hand of mobs. His friend dropped him at the Benapole. My father can see the tear was filled with Shen's eyes. Shen gave him a pack of Cigarettes and a hug. My dad said, "it was not expected." Shen said, "It was expected when Suhrawardy was elected as chief minister." His right hand "Khoka is a well-known goon."

In the late 40s, two political parties were Muslim League, and the Indian National Congress was the two largest political parties in British India. The Muslim League had demanded Pakistan, since its 1940 Lahore Resolution passed in the Muslim League Cabinet, that the

Reluctant Fathers

Muslim-majority areas of India in the Northwest and the East should make Pakistan.

In 1946 the British India Cabinet Mission to India for planning the transfer of power from the British Raj to the Indian leadership discussed three political structure possibilities: a center, groups of provinces, and provinces. The "groups of provinces" were meant to accommodate the Muslim League demand. Both the Muslim League and Congress, in principle, accepted the Cabinet Mission's plan. However, Muslim League speculated that Congress's acceptance was a political-strategic move rather than an objective.

After a lengthy discussion among Huseyn Shaheed Suhrawardy, Abul Kasem Fazlul Huq, Khwaja Nazimuddin, Abdus Sabur Khan, Nurul Amin, Kazi Qader, among many others, the meeting heavily debated the three states theory. Finally, Muslim League agreed that we are Muslim brothers. We must remain united as one Nation. Secondly, Banglastan would be inside a big non-Muslim country. The defense would be tough. Muslim League decided to fight for the two-nation theory.

In July 1946, Muslim League withdrew from the three states theory agreement with the Brith Government. Jinnah announced a general strike (hartal) on 16 August, known as Direct Action Day, to assert its demand for a separate homeland for Indian Muslims out of certain Northwestern and Eastern provinces in British India

Huseyn Shaheed Suhrawardy, right-hand man, Khoka, orchestrated a bloody communal riot in a closed-door meeting. The protest triggered massive bloodshed and loot in Calcutta. More than 4,000 innocent people lost their lives, and 100,000 residents were left homeless in Calcutta within three days. These riots spread to in Noakhali, Bihar, United Provinces, Punjab, and

Reluctant Fathers

the North-Western Frontier Province. This riot was an end for a United India. The religious hatred grows so deep that no leader knows how to control it.

On 14 August 1947, a new nation was born Pakistan under the Muslim League's leadership. Louis Francis Albert Victor Nicholas Mountbatten and Jinnah conspired to make Karachi Pakistan's capital and transferred power to Jinnah, declaring him as Governor-General. Mountbatten's excuse was Dhaka is too far from Bombay or Delhi. After the transfer of power, Pakistan can sort things out.

In 1948, Muslim League was divided into two Groups. Muslim League Jinnah the core principle of secularism and dominated by the Shia. Believes in British Crown is the Head of Pakistan and Governor-General.

Pakistan Muslim League's core principle is the Islamic Republic of Pakistan. Provincial Autonomy, two Pakistan, East and West, and central Government is the Islamic Republic of United Pakistan. The Head of United Pakistan Khalifa or President. The prime-ministership. Dhaka would be the Parliamentarian Capital, and West Pakistan would have a Presidential or Khalifat capital.

In June 1949, Muslim League was terrified, and that was the end of the Muslim League. A man, Abdul Hamid Khan Bhashani, who advanced the Muslim League movement in Bengal and Assam, decided to create a new political party, Awami Muslim League, the Muslim League's Gandhi. Without Abdul Hamid Khan Bhashani support Muslim League is nothing. Bhashani heart and mind of the poor Muslim in Bengal and Assam.

In 1950, East Pakistan Estate Acquisition Act 1950 greatly affected Hindu Zamindars and Muslim League Leaders because most Muslim Leaders were landowners. However, 80% of the estate (Zamindari) was Hindus.

Reluctant Fathers

In the 1954 election in East Bengal province of Pakistan, Muslim League suffers a heavy loss. My father managed to win his constituency. The socialists, Federalists, and Communists united front showed their muscle—end of Muslim League popularism.

In 1958 Ayub Khan took over. On the face of the Muslim Leaguers' smile returned. Pakistan Muslim League did not protest the Ayub Khan take over; instead, they welcome him. Muslim League Jinnah strongly opposed the military takeover. President Ayub Khan's era was a honeymoon time for Pakistan Muslim League. End up with humiliation.

In the 1970 election, Muslim League was wiped out in both Pakistan East and West. Pakistan Muslim League couldn't manage to have ten seats in United Pakistan. However, it was predicted that Muslim League would have more than a hundred seats due to speculation of Indian conspiracy and ongoing violence in the country. Muslim League voters confirmed the age between 40-60.

Nevertheless, the 1970 election outcome was due to various factors. After the 1970 cyclones in East Pakistan, the political situation changed dramatically. The pro-Mujib media capitalized on the cyclone and interpreted it as Pakistani sabotage against Bengali. After the East Pakistan Estate Acquisition Act 1950, Hindu Zamindars lost billions of dollars in East Pakistan assets. They were outraged. There were approximately fifteen thousand Hindu Zamindars who held more than 80% of the East Pakistan estate. They spread a rumor to their nearly fifty million former proza that Pakistanin wanted to enslave Bengalis that turned into a volcanic hatred between Bengalis and Pakistanis and Pakistani (Muslim League, Jamaat E Islami, Nejami Islami, Pakistan Democratic Party, Pakistan Communist Party, Pakistan Peoples Party, Pakistan Awami

49

(Federalist) Party). Despite the outcome, most political parties declared the Election was rigged by Yahya Khan, Mujibur Rahman eight party coalition, and Buttu. That was the end of the Muslim League.

Sher E Bengal

As History suggests, the Muslim bourgeois class formed Muslim League. There was a lack of poor Muslim representation in the party. As far as I know, there was not a written biography by Abul Kasem Fazlul Huq; therefore, it is challenging to define Abul Kasem Fazlul Huq's political agenda. I know for a fact the Abul Kasem Fazlul Huq was inspired by Karl Marx's political theory, and he relentlessly works toward socialism. And he strongly identified himself as a Muslim and willing to work with Muslim Leaguers. He is the founder of the Krishak Praja Party.

His party had two elements. No1. Krishak:- Krishak means those people who used to work for Muslim Malik/Mirasdar as farmers. The land belonged to Malik/Mirasdar. The Krishak work as a farmer and Mirasdar/Malik pays them for their work.No.2 Praja (Proza): Praja, according to the 1793 East India Company act, the Proza/Praja are technically slaves to the Zamindars.

The 1793 Act of East India Company intensified the anger between Muslim Malik/Mirasdar and Hindu Zamindars. In Islam, Muslims believe in brotherhood. Poor Muslims considered Fakir/ Miskin, not as a slave. The worker was known as Kamla. A well-known hadith known to all Muslim Lords that "Pay the worker his dues before his sweat has dried up" calling a free Muslim slave angered the Muslim bourgeois class.

However, Abul Kasem Fazlul Huq was invited to participate in the meeting to form Muslim League. In quest of negotiating with some founding members of Muslim Leaguers, Abul Kasem Fazlul Huq agreed to join with the Muslim Movement, but he never gave up his socialist agenda. Before the December 30 official declaration, Muslim League as a political representative for Muslims in British India, nearly three days leading Muslim Nawabs and Mirasdar discuss with Abul Kasem Fazlul Huq.

In 1930-31, Roundtable Conference, Abul Kasem Fazlul Huq unequivocally demanded a Muslim Independent state in front of the King that very moment he received the title from the famous Muslim poet Muhammad Iqbal and Dhaka Nawab "Sher E Bengal." On the contrary, Jinnah was busy with his 14 points loose Indian federalism.

On March 23, 1940, the All India Muslim League at Minto Park, in Lahore, by Sher E Bengal A.K. Fazlul Huq, presented a two-nation theory. Behind the scene, the so-called **Working Committee** was intensely debating on India's partition based on Hindu and Muslim, or Federal India, but Jinnah was a pain in the neck. He repeatedly points out his 14 points, whereas Jawaharlal Nehru, Subhas Chandra Bose, and Vallabhbhai Jhaverbhai Patel. Vallabhbhai Jhaverbhai Patel wanted a healthy centralized United Indian. In other words, one Indian policy. Jinnah had reliable support from Shia groups such as Aga Khan, which's why he could do a bit of monkey business.

In closed-door, the Sunni group told A.K. Fazlul Huq, "we trust your judgment." "You have a wealth of political experience, knowledge in the British and Islamic law." You guide us in this challenging moment. A.K. Fazlul Huq said, "Today or never," and He presented the two-nation theory. Jinnah's ego got hurt. He was not expecting A.K. Fazlul Huq's two-nation theory would be publicly declared. The Shia group got infuriated. Aga Khan has only one thing in his mind. The Muslims are not capable of running a country. The Crown should be the head of state.

If the Shia establishment did not distort Pakistan's history, A.K. Fazlul Huq is entitled to be the Father of Pakistan. And Pakistan would have been much more stable and prosperous. The right solution for Pakistan was A.K. Fazlul Huq's idea of three Pakistan becoming one Pakistan. East Pakistan and West Pakistan two wings. The federal government is the Islamic Republic of United Pakistan. The Federal Government only accounts for Foreign policy, Defense Ministry, Finance Ministry, Communication Ministry, and regional ministry.

Khwaja Nazimuddin

Khwaja Nazimuddin was born in a Nawab family. I disapprove of the Dhaka Nawab because Nawab used to be appointed by the Delhi Sultanate. Historically, Delhi Sultanate made administrative changes few times in the past, and the British government abolished the last Mugal Mirza Abu Zafar Siraj-ud-din Muhammad on September 21, 1857. Therefore, Dhaka Nawab was not a legitimate Muslim Nawab. They were appointed by the British. And Sunni Muslims never accepted the British Government as legitimate rulers of India.

However, Dhaka Nawab Nawab Sir Khwaja Salimullah Bahadur had one of the highest contributions for Muslims in East Bengal. He worked hard to unite Muslims in Dhaka, spent lots of money sake of Muslim interest. He laid the foundation for Dhaka University.

In short, Khwaja Nazimuddin was not a sincere political leader as Khwaja Salimullah. He was much more ambitious than a politician. He lined with Jinnah to make the British Crown head of the state and Governor-General.

They both were obsessed with the British the idea of Governor Generalship. But he did agree with the name "Islamic Republic of Pakistan" under the British Crown.

Huseyn Shaheed Suhrawardy

Huseyn Shaheed Suhrawardy was not a Muslim founding member or believed in Muslim League political strategy. In a sense, he was deeply rooted emotionally Muslim. His entire political career was a flip-flop. His political ambition grew after he met his right-hand man Khoka, Bangladeshi Bengali father of the nation. Without Huseyn Shaheed Suhrawardy and Mujib, Pakistan would have never been born. The Calcutta riot was engineered under his watch and shifted the debate in the British parliament.

Politically, Suhrawrday wanted federal Pakistan with provincial autonomy, unlike Jinnah. He believed in regional autonomy and limiting the federal government interference in the provincial internal political crisis. He said, " Pakistan should be recognized as the Independent Nation, not under the British Crown."

Reluctant Fathers

Jinnah

Muhammad Ali Jinnah is widely respected in Pakistan (West Pakistan 1955-1971). I have never been fond of Jinnah. I was inspired by Boro ma bedtimes stories about my grandfather's Muslim League political activism at my early age. Secondly, I was inspired by Prophet Muhammed's (PBUH) biography book (I forgot the exact name). In 1906 winter, my grandfather went to Dhaka by horse to Sylhet City to participate in the Muslim League's formation in Dhaka. How he used to invite Muslim Mirasdar/ Zamindars/ Malik/ in our Tongi (bungalow) to discuss Muslim League progress, or he used to go to Calcutta these stories were very dear to me.

I never heard a word about Jinnah in my childhood. If I remember correctly, I listened to it a few times. In my father's coffee table conversation with his friends in Sylhet, if anyone talks about Jinnah, My dad spontaneously responded " "Ekta Gaddaar." It means he had no respect in our family. I hardly remember in the Bangladeshi families gathering anyone talked about Jinnah with respect.

However, I have learned about Jinnah by hearing, reading, and watching on youtube. To me, he was not a dedicated, sincere political activist like George Washington or Nelson Mandela or like any other politically significant leader. He was just an opportunist and was waiting for the right opportunity to take advantage. At his early age, his father, Jinnahbhai Poonja, wanted him to be like an English man. He worked hard to make his son Jinnah a barrister. As commonsense, as ordinary families sacrifice a lot to give their children better lives, his father did the same. There

Reluctant Fathers

was nothing special about Jinnah except climbing the ladder of better lives.

When Jinnah was in London as a student, his curiosity and ambition led him to meet with Dadabhai Naoroji. Jinnah helped in Dadabhai Naoroji's election campaign in the UK, which was his entry into British politics. The first Asian, Dadabhai Naoroji., became a British MP by seeing an Indian Man, became British MP, boosting his British political confidence.

According to the India Congress Party History, Jinnah expressed his political ambition in India by attending the Congress's twentieth annual meeting in Bombay in December 1904. He ascertained his Indian nationalism on the principle of secularism with Mehta, Naoroji Gopal, Krishna Gokhale. He was known as a moderate Muslim young man.

In the late 1930s, Jinnah came to Muslim Leaguers to join in Muslim League, as far as I heard. Muslim League challenged his intention. He said, " Mohammed Iqbal wanted him to join with Muslim League." Jinnah's backbone political supporter was Aga Khan in Muslim League. Politically, Jinnah and Muslim League had big problems. Jinnah wanted to have a weak federal India by keeping the British Crown as Head of India, whereas Congress leaders Jawaharlal Nehru, Subhas Chandra Bose, and Vallabhbhai Jhaverbhai Patel. Vallabhbhai Jhaverbhai Patel wanted a healthy centralized United India. And Muslim League wanted an Independent Muslim Country.

The odds are very obvious. His father, Jinnahbhai Poonja, brainwashed Jinnah at his early age about the English people's superiority over Indians and Muslims. He can not get out of the box to think logically, with historical

55

knowledge, wisdom, and political mechanism except firmly believing that Muslims and Indians are backward.

Most Sunni upper-class and middle class in Bengal fought against British occupy to have an Independent Muslim country. Two different psychological differences between Suni Muslim League founding members and Jinnah. Jinnah was submissive to British superiority, and Sunni Muslim leaguers were fighters against British occupy. Jinnah was widely accused of being a British agent in Bengal. Nevertheless, in the middle of 1947, he succeeded in his egoist stubbornness, with Lord Mountbatten's help in the close door deal to make Karachi a capital, British Crown head of Pakistan. He would be the Governor-General. Jinnah was unbelievably obsessed with the title "Governor-General."

The senior Muslim League leaders were waiting in Dhaka to receive Lord Mountbatten. Of course, communication was challenging those days. The millennial and zoomers generation will never understand that. It was a breach of trust, highly dishonor to Muslim myrtle in Bengal those who had sacrificed their lives, believing that Bengal will be a free state from the British occupation one day. Jinnah will remain in Muslim in Bengal heart and mind a traitor opportunist.

Pakistan

On 23 June 1757, under the leadership of Major-General **Robert Clive**. The first British victory in **South Asia**, the battle helped the Company seize control of independent **Bengal**. The Shia and Hindu coalition government collapsed. The Sunni establishment was expecting a retaking of Bengal by the Delhi government from Mir, Jafar, and Lord Clive as Sunni Muslims as for

Reluctant Fathers

Delhi's help. Delhi's support never came until this day. On September 21, 1857, the Sunni Muslim government was abolished and replaced by the British Crown.

On May 1, 1793, the permanent settlement act made Hindu Raja/ Zamindars autonomous rulers in Bengal villages. From thereon, poor Muslims were systematically abused, humiliated, lynched by the Hindu Zamindars. In Sylhet, King (Raja) Nath, Chad and a few others assured my great, great grandfather that they wouldn't insult poor Muslims in their petty kingdom (Raja). After this act, hundreds of years of old harmony between Hindu and Muslim was over. A new tension and mistrust grows between Muslims and Hindu. Hindus began reporting to the Rajas/Zamindars about Muslims sacrificing cows, killing the snake, breaking black stone to build houses, marrying Hindu girls by converting to Islam, hiring Sudras as a Khamla (worker).

Several times, my great grandfather Muhammed Hasim met with Raja Girish Chandra Roy to solve these issues. All the time, he gave empty promises. He laughed and said, " these issues belong to Brahman, my Raj Kanoon like yours, not Mullah Fatwa." Now, the new enemy within. The Permanent Settlement Act gave newly formed Hindu Raja/ Zamindars the feeling that they will be Raja/Zamindars forever under East India Company's protection. These were the social issues in the Sylhet and Bengal, which led them to think for an Independent Muslim Country. They failed to realize that one day, the British have to go.

A well-known Bengali Muslim story is that on 18 November 1831, a military unit consisting of a cavalry unit and infantry unit led by Major Scott, Lieutenant Shakespeare, and Major Sutherland laid a siege on

Titumir's fort. Nothing of significance happened until the morning of 19 November 1831, when a concerted ammunition charge was mounted. The resistance was breached in about three hours when the fort gave way to cannons.

Titumir was stabbed to death, as were fifty fellow soldiers. About 800 others were arrested and trialed at Alipur Court; Golam Masum was hanged in front of the fort-ruins to set an example, and about 140 had to serve prison terms of varying lengths. The commanding officer of the British forces noted his opponent's bravery in dispatches and commented on bamboo's strength and resilience as a material for fortification since he had had to pound it with artillery for a surprisingly long time before it gave way. This story highlighted the inspiration of independent Muslim Bengal.

In British history, On 29 March 1857 at Barrackpore, Sepoy Mangal Pandey of the 34th Bengal Native Infantry attacked his officers. When his comrades were ordered to restrain him, they refused, but they stopped joining him in open revolt. Following these incidents, the British Government banned hiring soldiers from Bengal until further notice. This ban was the end of military recruitment in Bengal until the first world war.

The Bengal Tenancy Act 1885 infuriated Muslim Mirasdar/MalikLords). They began attacking British interests. In retaliation, the British Crown seizing Muslim Mirasdar/Malik property and auctioning the seized property for ninety-nine years lease to the Hindus as Zamindars with the promissory of financial loan and military support. Muslims Lords did not like to use the word "Proza" for the Muslim poor because, in Islam, we believe in Muslim Brothers instead of using the name

Reluctant Fathers

"fakir-Miskin." The British Crown declared a full-scale war against Muslim Mirasdar/Malik by characterizing them as rebellious terrorists. And banded Muslims going to the Masjid when the British Crown realized strong support from Hindus upper caste.

In late 1899, Lord Curzon expressed his desire to meet with Muslims noble Nawab, Mirasdar/ Malik unofficially. In the meeting, my great grandfather, Muhammed Hasim, explained to Lord Curzon the social stigma in Sylhet. He said, " there is no negotiation except independent Sylhet, or my sword have an answer." Lord Curzon smiled at my grandfather and said: " Mr. Mohammed, I did not invite you all to answer you with my sword as representative of the British Crown; I am here to hear your grief and concern." I make clear, " There will be no Independent of Bengal or Sylhet, but I can assure you if you put your sword down and come to the political process, the Bengal will be partitioned but no violence if you all promise that."

On 16 October 1905, Bengal was partitioned as West Bengal and East Bengal as Lord Curzon promised. Lord Curzon kept his promise. October 16, 1905, was a day of national mourning for Hindu Zamindars and Raja. Hindu fasted and observed a general strike. The Muslims were celebrating the news. The song " Amar Sonar Bangla," composed by Rabindranath Tagore, was sung by many. Many were seen walking barefoot to the Ganga singing Vande Mataram.

On record, December 30, 1906, Muslim League was formed as Muslims promised with Lord Curzon.

Reluctant Fathers

In 1911, the British Government revoked the partition of Bengal under pressure from wealthy Hindu people in business, Raja, and Zamindars. In 1911, the British India capital was shifted from Calcutta to Delhi, East and West Bengal was reunited. Assam, Bihar, and Orissa were separated to form a new province. On the same day, Muslim activists swore to have an Independent Muslim Bengal.

In 1935, the British Crown decided to introduce a democratic election system to defuse Hindu Muslim tensions in Bengal.

In the 1937 Election in Bengal, Muslim League and Krishak Praja Party created a coalition government by making Abul Kasem Fazlul Huq the first prime minister of Bengal.

On March 23, 1940, Abul Kasem Fazlul Huq indirectly declared a Muslim country's independence in the Indian subcontinent by delivering a two-nation theory. Congress leader Abul Kalam Ghulam Muhiyuddin Ahmed bin Khairuddin Al-Hussaini Azad, known as Maulana Azad, rejected the two-state theory and asked for Muslim unity for United India. Maulana Azad explicitly described Muslim disunity among Muslims between Shia, Sunni, Sufi, and Muslim communities' class system. He said, " Muslim country is not a realistic solution for India," but creating a "constitutional republic of India is the right solution for India." History proves Maulana Azad was right "Pakistan is not a solution for Muslim." It's a disease in the world.

Reluctant Fathers

On August 16, 1946, Calcutta Killings's result of Direct Action Day orchestrated by Jinnah without proper consultation with the working committee, a British intelligence agent, confirmed Jinnah that it would be difficult under the upcoming Governor-General to make Pakistan. It led to large-scale violence between Muslims and Hindus in the city of Calcutta in the Bengal province of British India.

On August 14, 1947, Jinnah created Pakistan in a closed-door conspiracy between Jinnah and Mountbatten. In my opinion, Jinnah could not control his greed to become a Governor-General. A title that he highly admired and deep respect for the British Crown. Jinnah found the opportunity to play a monkey business with Muslim Leaguers because Bombay and Dhaka's distance and poor communication and healthy backers were wealthy Shia.

On September 11, 1948, Jinnah died. He left Pakistan in uncertain territory. Politically unstable religious strife between Hindu-Muslim top of that he created a regional tension between Bengali and Urdu speaking, an unsettled constitutional crisis. Economic uncertainty. A question needs to ask, how he became a father when he left massive political, social, economic, religious, regional problems on the shoulder of a new nation?

President Ayub Khan

On October 27, 1958, Army General from West Pakistan declared a military takeover. Pakistan Muslim League (Sunni stronghold) sunshine on their face. They quickly welcomed Ayub Khan and exclaimed, "Pakistan saved." Muslim League (Jinnah) condemn the military takeover. Pakistan Muslim League and Ayub Khan made excellent political relationships. Ayub Khan used to respect the traditional Muslim Leaguers highly. And he was taking political advice from them.

In reality, the Ayub Khan takeover was a necessity. Between 1947-1958, Pakistan was suffering a political crisis. East Pakistan had powerful support for socialism, the Islamic Republic of Pakistan with provincial autonomy. An insignificant Muslim Leaguers (Jinnah), mostly Aga Khani, wanted to reinstate Governor-General under the British Crown.

Pakistan Muslim League wanted the Islamic Republic of Pakistan with provincial semi-autonomy. And full independence from the British Crown.

My father's advice was to President Ayub Khan implement a basic democracy to train our people in the election because they were hundreds of years Hindu proza and do not understand the politics. By creating a Village governmental system, they will learn how to develop their villages. President Ayub Khan expressed concern about the cost. He said, " that would be highly costly" instead, he created more than five thousand Union Presidency in East Pakistan.

During President Ayub Khan Presidency, Pakistan's economy took its peak. Brilliant Muslim Leaguers advised President Ayub Khan to focus on industrialization, education, and agriculture. The rapid development of Pakistan, the envious British Crown, and India could not digest it. British Intelligence Agent, Thomas Williams, wrote six points on paper and handed them to Mujib. Mujib was under legal cases brought by the martial administration; Mujib's primary mentor Huseyn Shaheed Suhrawardy passed away on December 5, 1963. That's why he was looking for an expert lawyer. Mujib's close friend

Reluctant Fathers

Tazuddin Ahmed advised him to go to London to find an expert lawyer to help him. In East Pakistan, there is no legal expert in martial law cases. Instead, Mujib came with six points on his hand in East Pakistan.

Mujib and Tajuddin significantly discuss the merit of the six-points. Tazuddin told Mujib that the six-point would help Awami League open a negation on the provincial autonomy instead of one unit government. Secondly, it will divert the martial law administrator to continue his fraudulent financial cases on the court.

August – 23 September 1965, Indo-Pak War was a blunder mistake by President Ayub Khan. East Pakistan was left vulnerable to Indian aggression, the conversation in East Pakistan Muslim middle class dramatically changed. They lost confidence in Ayub Khan's one unit government. The Awami League took this conversation as a political opportunity.

On February 5, 1966, Mujib placed six points before the subject committee's meeting and urged to include the issue in the next day's conference agenda. The committee rejected the six-points, and Sheikh Mujibur Rahman was characterized as a separatist element.

On May 8, 1966, Mujib was arrested under the Defence of Pakistan act, an unfounded case accused of Agartala Conspiracy. The Awami League interpreted the arrest as silencing the voice of underrepresenting Bengali.

On February 22, 1969, Sheikh Mujibur Rahman, the All-Pakistan Awami League leader, was released in an unsettled court-martial case. Dhaka University students declared him "Bongobondhu."

On March 25, 1969, President Ayub Khan resigned from the Presidency with humiliation in East Pakistan and West Pakistan. Once he was highly admired in United

Reluctant Fathers

Pakistan, who won Pakistan's nickname saver, he left Pakistan under the brink of breaking Pakistan.

Mujib

Talking about Mujib is highly dangerous. Bangladeshi Bengali highly revered him. If you speak about Mujib in Bangladesh, your life would be in great danger. High possibility of a subject of a targeted killing.

According to the BBC 2004 polls, the BBC announced Sheikh Mujibur Rahman, the Greatest Bengali of all time, voted by Bengalis worldwide.

In late 2011, As Journalist Sagar Sarowar and I discussed creating an informative Debunk 71 documentary Youtube movie. On the morning of February 11, 2012. He and his wife were murdered in his Dhaka residency. The Bangladesh Government did not do a thorough criminal investigation. His murder is proof that it is impossible to talk or write about the pro and con of 1971 and Mujib in Bangladesh.

However, I will briefly tell you about Mujib. In the late 40s, Mujib used to bring tea in the Huseyn Shaheed Suhrawardy office during the Muslim League Leaders coffee table conversation or meetings. During the Hindu-Muslim riot, Mujib looted Hindu wealthy families' wealth. He used to know Hindu wealthy families because his father was a tea boy in a prominent Hindu lawyer office. After the creation of Pakistan, he built a big house with the looted money in Dhaka.

In 1948, he managed to have a fake college certificate admitted to Dhaka University. Still, Dhaka University identified a fraudulent certificate. He was expelled from the university at the request of Huseyn

Reluctant Fathers

Shaheed Suhrawardy. The Dhaka university reversed the decision and made it rusticate because Huseyn Shaheed Suhrawardy needed Mujib for his political interest in the Faridpur district. According to the ethics committee, an expelled student from the university on the ground of fraud will automatically disqualify Mujib to run for Assembly Faridpur; that's the exact reason Huseyn Shaheed Suhrawardy wanted a political rusticate for Mujib not expelled on the ground of fraud.

According to the East Pakistan financial banking fraudulent case, Mujib had twenty fraudulent bank loan documents where he claimed he is the minister of twenty East East ministries. In 1954, provincial election Mujib elected in the Provincial Assembly that Government lasted approximately two years.

During 1948-66, Mujib helped thousands of Bengali people to take Hindu abandoned houses by threatening Hindus; his group earned the nickname Mujib Bhahini. He also helped Dhaka University students to find lodges or roommates. At the university, he was nicknamed "Mujib Vehi." That's how he won the heart and mind of the Bengali people in Dhaka. In reality, he was a goon.

1970 Election

Regarding the 1971 war, the Bangladeshi Bengali and Pakistan military are pathological liars. Bangladeshi Bengali and Pakistan army spreading too much lie about the 1971 war. Bangladeshi Bengali is systematically brainwashing Bangladeshi messes that 1971 war was Bengali Unified Bangladesh Independent movement for the Bangladesh Independent. First and foremost, both

Reluctant Fathers

Bangladeshi and Pakistani need to acknowledge that the war's root cause was the 1970 election. The 1970 election was highly controversial between political parties. Some Pakistani political parties ask for the election boycott due to the November 3, 1970, national cyclone disaster. Some did not want to participate in the 1970 election under military rule. Muslim League council, Awami league senior leaders, and Awami Bhashani(Socialist) strongly criticized President Yahya Khan. for mishandling the cyclone disaster. Awami Bhashani interpreted the mishandling of the cyclone as discrimination against East Pakistani Bengali.

However, Awami Mujib welcomed the election. Upon accepting the general election for National Assembly and provincial Assemble, Mujib agreed that a constitution would be written and ratified by all provinces after a United Pakistan election.

During the negotiation, Mujib did not admit that he wanted a confederation Union or independent country. The well-documented fact that he said his six points are only a political bargain with President Ayub Khan because of his one unit presidential system and dictatorial rule. Mujib swears by the Quran that he will not break Pakistan and respect the ratified new constitution when elected representatives pass it with the majority vote.

It must be noted that between 1967-1970 Dhaka was under the Mujib Bahini. Mujib's stronghold was Dhaka University. Unfortunately, Nawab Salimullah built Dhaka University, which Muslim League lobbied to give higher education to Muslims in East Bengal, Assam, Tripura but Mujib made it a mini-cantonment 1948-56 and 1966-1970. A commonsense question, Mujib was not a Dhaka

University student; why did he almost every evening hang out in Madhur Canteen? Logically speaking, he was exploiting Dhaka University students for his political ambition. One of Mujib's good things was finding logging or a roommate for remote villagers' new students at Dhaka University. These students were Mujib's political asset at the 1970 election. They emotionally supported Mujib, spread all the rumors and lies, and filled up the empty ballot box with ballots.

As most all Bangladeshi Bengali proudly argue, the 1970 election was a referendum on Bangladesh. I understand their lack of knowledge due to various factors such as family background and disinformation. In 1970 not even five percent of East Pakistani used to know how to read or write because of the two hundred years of Hindu Zamindars slavery.

My father and relatives were political candidates for the National and provincial Assembly; therefore, I have heard all the issues about the 1970 election. The new generation knew nothing about the election. They only know Pakistani wanted to enslave Bengalis and systematically abused them; in other words, Pakistanis are invaders. That's why Bengali wanted Independence from Pakistan. Pakistani is a curse to most Bengali. That's not the case. East Pakistani was a majority, and East Pakistan was thousands of miles away from West Pakistan. Originally, East Pakistani Muslims created Pakistan in 1946, and it was seeded in 1911.

The 1971 War

The 1971 war is a mystery or tragedy or liberation or Independence or a successful intelligence operation, or a civil war or a betrayal depends on whom you ask. The War

Reluctant Fathers

General MAG Osmani used to call it a "mystery." He did not know anything about the 71 war until at the end of April entered India. To my father, it was a betrayal of the Pakistan military. To the Communist Party, it's a political-strategic mistake because the Communist Party wanted a communist revolution in United Pakistan. It's liberation to Bangladeshi Nationalist's Party because their leader Major Zia revolted against Pakistani military searchlight operation to save East Pakistanis from upcoming an army atrocity in East Pakistan. To RAW, it was a successful intelligence operation A-Z. To most Awami Leaders, it's a tragedy because they were preparing for Federalism with provincial autonomy.

However, there were three groups inside of the Awami League. No. 1, Old Awami, they always wanted Federalism with provincial autonomy. They were the founding members of the Awami Muslim League and previously were Muslim Leaguers. No.2, Awami Bhashani is known as National Awami Party (NAP), is a socialist ideological party that wanted socialism in Pakistan. No.3, Awami Mujib Bahini consisted of Dhaka University Students, Hindu Minority, RAW Agents, and Dhaka's famous goons.

In Dhaka during 1948-1966, Mujib was a well-known goon. He earned the nickname "Mujib Vahi." Between 1948-66, Mujib used to be hired to invade Hindu abandoned properties. Regularly, people used to hire Mujib for land disputes and invasion. His legal and political shelter was Huseyn Shaheed Suhrawardy.

Dhaka University Students made Mujib a political icon in 1969. They declared him "Mujib Vahi" to "Bangabandhu." Mujib used to help Dhaka university

Reluctant Fathers

students to find lodging, roommate, admission fees, and food. Most of the students used to come from remote villages, and Mujib Vahi was their only hope. It is well-documented that all the Dhaka University student's Government-elected leaders had lunch or dinner in Mujib house almost every day.

In reality, Mujib legitimately never was a Dhaka University student. Mujib managed to have a fraudulent certificate to be admitted to Dhaka University. The Dhaka University board identified the fraudulent certificate. He was expelled from the university at the request of Huseyn Shaheed Suhrawardy. The Dhaka university reversed the decision and made it rusticate because Huseyn Shaheed Suhrawardy needed Mujib for his political interest. According to the ethics committee, an expulsion from the university on the ground of fraud will automatically disqualify Mujib to run for Assembly; that's the exact reason Huseyn Shaheed Suhrawardy wanted a political rusticate for Mujib.

However, Mujib was a goon, not a politician. He did not create the Bangladesh independence movement, nor he knew the name "Bangladesh." There is no authentic information regarding Mujib's involvement in creating the Bangladesh movement except the Agartala Conspiracy meeting. In the meeting, Mujib never expressed his desire for an Independent Country. Tajuddin Ahmad tried to convince Mujib for Independence in the discussion. According to the authentic source of information, the mastermind behind creating Bangladesh was I.B. Agent Serajul Alam Khan code name (DADA).

There were four groups of people who were actively engaged with creating the Bangladesh independence

Reluctant Fathers

movement. And lead the East Pakistan war with West Pakistan. No. 1, RAW agents, according to the authentic source of information, after the 1965 war, Ms. Indira Priyadarshini Gandhi vowed an oath to kill the snake. After she won the 1966 election, she invited only three trusted people in a secret room for a confidential meeting, colonel Nanon (code name), Journalist Banerjee (code name), and red flag (code name). I guess that the red flag was Jyoti Basu. Until 1968, the Intelligence Bureau (I.B.), responsible for India's internal intelligence, also handled external intelligence. But after India's miserable performance in a 1962 border war with China, the need for a separate external intelligence agency was apparent. During that conflict, "our intelligence failed to detect Chinese build-up for the attack," writes Maj. Gen. VK Singh, a retired army officer who did a stint in RAW, No.2, Hindu Minority. Hindu minority in East Pakistan and Dhaka had a profoundly painful experience during 1946-1966. Their houses were looted, women were raped, and Mujib Bahini forcefully took Hindu lands. The Hindu Zamindars and traders used to own more than eighty percent of the land in East Pakistan. Their anger and burning for revenge exploded in 1969-1971.

No.3, Dhaka University students were crucial for the 1971 war. That's why Pakistan's military-first attack at Dhaka University in the middle of the night on March 25, 1971. In 1969 the anti-Ayub student movement turned into a chaotic situation. Awami Bhashani demanded the immediate release of Mujib as noted Mujib was arrested for Agartala Conspiracy. I.B. Agent Serajul Alam, Khan code name (DADA), advised Bhashani and student leaders to fight for Mujib release unitedly. The Dhaka University Students declared Mujib "Bangabandhu." And throw a nuclear bomb in the crowd, "Joy Bengala," that exploded in the student movement and shook the nation. The "Joy Bangla" and "Joy Bangabandhu" rapidly spread in every school and college; these two phrases of slogan advanced the Bangladesh independence movement for more than a hundred years.

No.4, The goons of East Pakistan used the 1969-71 political situation as an opportunity to loot, rape, murder, land invasion among Hindu and Muslim activists in the name of Mujib. Law and order collapsed. Mujib publicly declared that East Pakistan runs on his command. Not on Yahya Khan's command. The political, social, and religious situation deteriorated so that there was no saver for the country.

In 1969, President Ayub Khan was advised to hand over power to a Civilian patriot. He refused and handed it to Yahya Khan. That was a blunder by President Ayub Khan. Well-documented that General Yahya Khan is commonly drunk all the time. General Yahya Khan built a political coalition with Mujib, Butto, Jamaat-E- Islami, Nejami Islami and ignored socialists and Muslim League. In contrast, Muslim League Leaders were President Ayub Khan's right-hand political mentors since 1958.

Reluctant Fathers

Countdown to The 71 War

On February 22, 1969, Sheikh Mujibur Rahman, the All-Pakistan Awami League leader, walked out free from bizarre imprisonment from the Dhaka army cantonment. Thousands of his supporters escorted him to his Dhanmondi residence, for that was an emotional reunion with his families and supporters.

On May 8, 1966, Mujib was arrested under the Defence of Pakistan act, an unfounded case accused of Agartala Conspiracy. A civilian, in a bizarre court-martial law trial procedure in the history which he, along with thirty-four other conspirators (men in the armed forces and the civil administration), had been charged with conspiracy to have East Pakistan seceded from the rest of United Pakistan through an armed revolt with Indian military assistance. It was argued by the Government of Field Marshal Mohammad Ayub Khan that Mujib had earlier traveled to Agartala in India to solicit Indian support for his scheme of breaking up United Pakistan.

The Agartala Conspiracy was first leaked in early December 1965 by a small newspaper Daily Nishan, Malibag, Dhaka. The newspaper could not detail the Agartala meeting's exact nature, but it stated that "A New Country is about to Born.". Pakistan's Intelligence (ISI) tried to get the authenticity of the report. But, the editor declined to reveal the name of the source of information. But, he hints that the Awami Mujib group.

Reluctant Fathers

Pakistan's Government remained quiet about the Agartala meeting; indeed, President Ayub breaks the silence in 1966, as soon after Mujib had announced his Six-Point plan for confederation autonomy within a federal Pakistan, to the effect that those who supported the six-point movement would be considered as the enemy of Pakistan and will deal with under the Defence of Pakistan Act. That announcement hit the Headlines of all the Newspapers in East Pakistan. That was a billion dollars worth of free publicity for Awami Mujib.

The unsettled Agartala conspiracy case made Mujib's name famous overnight in East Pakistan. And excellent free publicity for the 6 points. In villages, the illiterate people started spreading made-up stories and gossip in the tea-stalls and college students in the college cafeterias about the Mujib and his six-points. Now, Mujib is an unstoppable movement.

All Parties Roundtable Meetings

In 1969, President Ayub Khan invited all the political parties from East Pakistan and West Pakistan for a sustainable political solution for a United Pakistan, known as the "Round Table Conference." In the meeting, the Jamaat Islami leader, Abul A'la Maududi, proposed a ninety-day caretaker governmental system to conduct a free and fair election. The United Pakistan Muslim League opposed the idea of a caretaker government and demanded hand over power to an East Pakistan General fear of Indian aggression and appease the East Pakistani movement. The All-Pakistan Awami League party pressed a hand over power to a civilian patriot as Pakistan's military wishes. The Pakistan Peoples Party, led by Zulfikar Ali Bhutto, refused to attend the roundtable conference. Instead, he demanded the immediate resignation of President Ayub Khan. However, he asked for a robust anti-Ayub demonstration all over the country.

In 1969 in East Pakistan, Dhaka University Students, Awami Bhasani and Mujib's Bhahini, the local goons, created a tsunami of violence, riots, loot, murder, and rape daily routine. The Police force in East Pakistan declared a callose of law and order. In a Public meeting, Mujib stated that he is the de facto ruler of East Pakistan.

In 1969 in West Pakistan, The Pakistan Peoples Party (PPP) led powerful Anti- Ayub Khan protests, street demonstrations, and riots against the Ayub Khan's Government. When the prices hiked on the food consumer products such as sugar, tea, and wheat, people widely disapproved of Ayub Khan's Government by chanting slogans "Dowan to Ayub Khan." and employing insults to refer to Ayub. On the streets of West Pakistan's major cities, there was massive wall chalking that identified as derogatory and pejorative terms used on Ayub and his defaming image that made headlines in the West Pakistan news media. The Home and Defence Minister Vice-Admiral Rahman told the journalists that the "country was under the Mob rule and that Police were not strong enough to tackle the situation."

President Ayub Khan Resign

On March 25, 1969, President Ayub Khan resigned from Presidency and handed power to the army General Yahya Khan's commander-in-chief to bring stability to the country. He immediately imposed martial law and promised a fair and free election after restoring law and order in East Pakistan and West Pakistan.

Reluctant Fathers

General Yahya Khan's Presidency & War 71

On March 25, 1969, General Yahya Khan was inaugurated as a President of United Pakistan. He imposed martial law administration declaring martial law nationwide by guaranteeing free and fair election, ratifying a new constitution, and handing over the power to a newly elected civilian head of state, whether President or Prime-Minister. He inherited a two-decade of constitutional crisis in the country.

And the inter-provincial racial tension between the Punjabi-Pashtun-Mohajir dominating West Pakistan and the ethnically-Bengali-Bihari(Mohajir) and Punjabi in East Pakistan. It needs to be noted, Jinnah created regional hatred in 1948. The first problem he began by declaring Pakistan as a secular state, whereas Pakistan was created based on Muslim Nationalism. He was advised to form the Islamic Republic of Pakistan instead of centralization based on secularism. He boastfully disrespects all the senior Muslim Leaguer's advice and arrogantly declared a secular state of Pakistan that was a big blow to the Pakistan Unity. Muslim League lost popularity and never regain the same popularity until this day.

Some Muslim Leaguers broke up with the Muslim League because of arrogant Jinnah. In June 1949, Awami Muslim League was formed under Abdul Hamid Khan Bhashani, Bhashani, in his speech during the Awami Muslim League formation. He said, "Awami Muslim League is a Sallam (Goodbye) to Jinahism, not Muslimism." the Muslim League council (Khwaja Nazimuddin), my father was with this group struggled to reunite the Muslim League. But, everyone was cursing Jinnah for the chaos in Muslim League.

Secondly, Jinnah gave a speech to make "Urdu would be Pakistan's official language." He publicly declared, "whoever opposes the idea that they are an enemy of Pakistan." He did not give anyone a chance to debate the issue of language democratically. It was outright a dictatorial speech. The problems were already made by Jinnah and only passed it to President Yahya Khan.

President Yahya Khan tried to solve Pakistan's constitutional crisis by returning to the pre-1958 political structure. The political decision was correct, but it was too late, and no return. A systematic approach was needed to defuse the political violence, write a new constitution and make a referendum. That would have served two purposes. No. 1, divert public attention from street demonstration and protest to open a political college-cafeteria, corner tea stall, and living room coffee table conversation No.2, return the normal economic vibration.

However, the Centralized Government dissolution did not bring a positive outcome to both East Pakistan and West Pakistan that might have happened earlier. President Yahya Khan abolished the parity principle, hoping that a more significant share for East Pakistan in the Assembly would satisfy the East Pakistani ethnic, regional majority and ensure Pakistan's Unity. Instead of fulfilling the Bengalis, it intensified violence, loot, target killings, and rape.

Cyclone Bhola 1970

The 1970 Bhola cyclone was a devastating tropical cyclone that struck East Pakistan and India's West

Reluctant Fathers

Bengal on November 11, 1970. It was one of the deadliest tropical cyclones ever recorded and one of the world's deadliest natural disasters. Most political parties demanded suspension of the November general election and helped the people. But Mujib asked for the postponement of the election.

The various sources and authentic information are that Chittagong DC informed President Yahya Khan that the situation is under control. Some of the minor incidents hear that President Yahya Khan canceled the trip to Chittagong and accepted Mujib's demand to postpone the election. In reality, The DC was under gunpoint by the Awami goons to prevent President Yahya Khan's visit to Chittagong so that Awami could capitalize on the Cyclones Disaster for their political advantage.

Awami's politicization of the cyclone was one of the heinous crimes committed by the Awami League. It was an unforgivable sin. There should be a criminal investigation on the 1970 cycle in East Pakistan; the disinformation created a volcanic hatred between East Pakistan and West Pakistan.

1970 General Elections

On July 28, 1969, President Yahya Khan formulated a general elections framework for United Pakistan to be held in November 1970. Due to a cyclone disaster in East Pakistan, On the demand of Awami Mujib, the election was postponed to December 7, 1970. to elect members of the National Assembly.

Reluctant Fathers

The highly controversial election was held on December 7, 1970. It was the first general election in Pakistan History. And only ones held as United Pakistan. Voting took place in 300 constituencies, of which 162 were in East Pakistan and 138 in West Pakistan.

My father was a candidate for National Assembly from Muslim League Council. Until his death, he always maintained that the election was rigged. In our village voting center, not even ten people cast their vote. But, the Awami League candidate won a high number of votes in my father's constituency. My father said all the highschool and college kids sealed the ballots instead of the rightful voters.

We need to understand that our people were illiterate, and women were not allowed to go outside of the houses without valid reasons. Women going out was a shameful act. And they were going to cast a vote that was beyond imagination. However, my father sent a few trusted women to investigate fourteen villages to know if women were voting or not. There were hardly any respected Muslim family women who voted except some poor women. One woman told my dad she sealed one hundred ballot books for a few hundred Taka.

The general election was held all over United Pakistan. In East Pakistan, the Awami League, led by Mujibur Rahman, held almost all seats but no seats in West Pakistan's four provinces. The socialist Pakistan Peoples Party (PPP) had won the exclusive mandate in the four provinces of West Pakistan but none in East Pakistan. The Pakistan Democratic League (PDL), led by Nurul Amin, won a one-seat in East Pakistan and zero seats in West Pakistan., was the only non-Awami party to have representation from East Pakistan. Still, it had failed to gain the mandate to create a coalition Government. The Awami

Reluctant Fathers

League had 160 seats that gave them absolute political right to form a government for five years, which all won from East Pakistan. The socialist PPP 81 gained enough seats to be an opposition party for five years, and the conservative PML 10 seats in the National Assembly disqualified them from being an opposition party.

The general elections' result was a severe political crisis for United Pakistan. The fear and anxiety increase among Muslim Leaguers. Muslim Leaguers were obnoxious about Mujib for many reasons as far as I heard from some Muslim League leaders; these are: No. 1, Mujib Agartala conspiracy case unsettled. No.2, Mujib 6 points. Mujib never publicly acknowledged who authored it. No.3, Mujib had 20 financial Bank fraud exceptional cases. He wrote on the loan application that he is the provincial minister for 20 ministries. He was elected only once for a few months. No. 4, inexperience in the administrative duties. No.5, He was a goon in Dhaka known as Mujib Bahini. Some criminal cases were pending. No.6, Indian interference. Etc.

The general election was a dead-end for United Pakistan. Several trilateral political negotiations were made between Zulfikar Ali Bhutto, President Yahya Khan, and Mujibur Rahman to create a coalition government to show unity to Pakistan's counterpart India. By delaying the transfer of power, cause more violence and bloodshed on the streets of Dhaka. President Yahya Khan indirectly asked Mujib by a piece of source information to know Mujibs motive "does he want an Independent country as most generals and Muslim League fearing about?". The answer was absolute No. He directly told the informant that the situation is not under his control because he is under overwhelmed pressure from the students. The only way he can control the crowd by opening the parliament is that

President Yahya was afraid to hand over the power to Mujibs because of underlying causes.

On March 1, 1971, The National Assembly was supposed to assemble in the parliament; instead, President Yahya declared martial law for an indefinite period that's the end of hope for a united Pakistan. Delhi already made Bangladesh. No, U-turn.

Flag Hoisted

On March 2, 1971, the flag was hoisted in Bangladesh for the first time at Dhaka University by student leader A. S. M. Abdur Rab, the then Vice President of Dhaka University Students' Union (DUCSU). According to the intelligence, The flag of Bangladesh was created by the I.B. Agent Serajul Alam Khan code name (DADA) instruction.

1971 intelligence briefing to some Muslim League leaders by the request of former President Ayub Khan was authentic. I have checked on wikipedia.org to verify the Bangladeshi Bengalis' proud admission of the 71 war conspiracy.

According to Wikipedia, as of January 13, 2021, the first version of the flag was designed and made by a section of student leaders and Swadheen Bangla Nucleus's activists on June 6, 1970, 108 Iqbal Hall (now Sergeant Zahurul Haq Hall). Dhaka University; students involved with the design were Kazi Aref Ahmed, ASM Abdur Rab, Shahjahan Siraj, Manirul Islam (Marshal Moni), Swapan Kumar Choudhury, Quamrul Alam Khan Khasru, Hasanul Haq Inu, and Yousuf Salahuddin

Ahmed. The flag was made from clothes donated by Bazlur Rahman Lasker, Apollo Tailors, Dhaka New Market.

All the intelligence suggests that India was preparing for a proxy war with Pakistan in East Pakistan by using Dhaka University students. Nevertheless, Dhaka University students were a great asset for the proxy war.

As my study showed that I.B. Agent Serajul Alam Khan code name (DADA) orchestrated a war in the middle of 1970 that was known to everyone giving the election was a blunder mistake. Even Serajul Alam Khan (DADA) admitted in Jackson Height in New York to me that he is the father of Bangladesh and Mujib was his doll. And also, Barrister Moudud Ahmed admitted Dada met with Ms. Indira Gandhi. All the evidence suggests that war was inevitable. The election and negotiation were a waste of time.

7th March Speech

The March 7, 1971 speech of Sheikh Mujibur Rahman at the Ramna Race Course Field in Dhaka is highly controversial between Bangladeshi Bengali Nationalists and Bangladeshi Nationalists and also Bangladesh Communist Party. Bangladeshi Bengali claimed March 7 speech is a declaration of Independence, whereas Bangladeshi Nationalist Party (BNP) and Bangladeshi Communist Party reject that.

Background of the 7th March speech I found very interesting as Bangladesh founder Serajul Alam Khan rightly said, "মুজিবুর একটি পুতুল" (Mujib is a Doll). When President Yahya Khan heard that Mujib is going to give a speech, he and some Muslim Leaguer send few informants to find out if Mujib was going to declare Independence or not. Mujib ensured Dhaka Muslim League Leader Kazi Qader and M A Yousuf that he would not declare Independence; instead, he emphasized that he also gave blood for the Pakistan movement.

He said the only way to prevent the Independence movement is the transfer of power. There are no alternatives. He can not control the crowd; the students are not listening to him; instead, they are pressuring him to declare Independence. He is not hiding anything. Muslim League and the generals do not want that. They do not wish Mujib as President or Prime-Minister of Pakistan.

Before March 7 night, students and Tazuddin created tremendous pressure on Mujib to declare Independence. Mujib stands still not to declare Independence; instead, he is ready for his arrest. After the March 7th speech, Mujib was continuously negotiating with President Yahya Khan until his arrest on March 25. Mujib was expecting his arrest sitting on his sofa. Finally, the military came and arrested him.

Searchlight Operation March 25

Operation Searchlight was conducted in the middle of March 25, 1971, known as কাল রাত্রির (blackout night); it was one of the worst preplanned miscalculated military genocide against the Hindu minority and rebellious students in East Pakistan. During that night, my father was in Dhaka Continental Hotel for a meeting with Muslim League Leaders. In early March, he went to Dhaka from Sylhet to discuss its political development with Muslim League Leaders. Dhaka is approximately one hundred fifty miles from Sylhet; that's why he decided to stay a couple of weeks in the hotel.

Reluctant Fathers

If I remember correctly, I heard from my father's conversation with his friends that my father went to sleep after Isha's prayer in his hotel room. In late-night, he listened to some gunfire. He woke up drinking a glass of water, went to the bathroom to make **wudu**. He was praying two Rakat in the meantime somebody knocked on the door. He asked, "who is disturbing me in the middle of the night?". Somebody answered, "I am a Muslim Leaguer from Chittagon district, "Lal Saab, please, open the door" (some people used to call my father Lal, Saab, Vehi).

When he opened the door, he saw a dozen Pakistani soldiers standing at the front of his room door. He shouted, "how dare, Mr. Yahya, to arrest me in the middle of the night..I have to sleep now". A military officer advanced his hand to shake my father's hand. Handshaking is a Muslim culture. He said that "moulvi Saab, I am a colonel, so and so" we are here not to arrest you but ask you to leave Dhaka immediately. We have intelligence that Indian militaries are hiding in the Dhaka University rooms to train students in a guerrilla war. President cares for your safety and security. That's why we are here to take you to the train station. The military Jeep will drop you off at the kamalapur train station. You can take the early morning train to Sylhet. My father said, "that's fine; let me get ready." The military Jeep with my dad a few other Muslim Leaguers dropped off at the kamalapur train station.

My father said that that night Dhaka was relatively quieter than the other nights. The train was pretty empty compared to other days. He was regretting having a cabin with his colleagues. My dad said to his colleagues that "Tikka Khan made the third-class a first-class reason why we are wasting money here." Chittagong Muslim League Leader Muslauddin noted, "we are not paying for this train fare; the military paid for us." My dad said, Muslauddin

Reluctant Fathers

Saab, this time the military is paying for us; it is not a good thing; the Indian army can attack us anytime. " The Pakistani military needs funds to fight the enemy." Muslauddin nodded "affirmatively."

In 1971, coming from Dhaka to Sylhet by train, the military put my dad on a Chittagong train. He had to change the train at the Akhaura Junction to Sylhet's local train. He got off at the Maijgaon Train Station. My maternal grandparent's village is in Maijgaon, KM Tilla. He went to my grandparents' house instead of going to his town. Before he went to Dhaka, he left my mother with her family Majigaon. After a couple of weeks, he returned home with my mom by boat.

According to my father's count, Akhaura Junction was an ongoing daily lifestyle. People were going about their life. But there was a strong military presence around Akhaura Junction because Akhaura Junction has a close border with India. In Maijgaon, people were talking about various kinds of stuff. Some said "a major revolt and killing lots military like a mad man," some said "Indian Army already in Dhaka." Etc.

The hearsay in the villages were illogical gossip and made-up stories. There was no substantial evidence to prove the village people gossip related to the 25th March operation. The remote villages did not have enough information because there was no radio, tv, or newspapers. Even if there was a local newspaper, only a number of people knew how to read. That's why they were spreading all the baseless rumors.

According to the pro-Pakistani elements, the widespread violence resulting from anti-Ayub lead to

Reluctant Fathers

Operation Searchlight led to the Bangladesh Liberation War. My research showed otherwise. The architect of Bangladesh Serajul Alam Khan, his word he was walking toward Bangladesh Independence way before Mujib's six-point.

      Searchlight operation did anger the Muslim Leaguers without any doubt. They felt like they beat the Hell out of the military. Even MAG Osmani, the War General, was a hardcore Pakistani and Muslim Nationalist. He became a War General for the 71 war because of the massacre.

Reluctant Fathers

The Serajul Alam Khan's War

There is sizable evidence that the Bangladesh Independence was first organized in Agartala by Tazuddin Ahmed, known as the Agartala conspiracy. Secondly, it was organized in Dhaka University under Serajul Alam Khan's leadership on June 6, 1970.

According to the authentic source of documentary evidence, the searchlight master plan was created in March 1971 by Major General Khadim Hussain Raja, GOC 14th Division. Major General Rao Farman Ali's follow-up of decisions taken at a meeting of the Pakistan Army staff on February 22. The 16th infantry division from Quetta and the 9th division from Kharian, West Pakistan, were ordered to prepare to move to East Pakistan in mid-February also due to that meeting.

Some Pakistan senior military officers were unwilling to support the searchlight operation on civilians' disregard Hindu or Muslim. Lt. General Shahabzada Yakub Khan, GOC East Pakistan, and East Pakistan's governor, Vice Admiral Syed Mohammad Ahsan, were relieved of their duties because he refused to execute the Operation. Lt. Gen. Tikka Khan took the Governorship and GOC of East Pakistan.

On March 17, General Raja was given the order to execute the Operation by telephone by General Abdul Hamid Khan, Chief of Staff of the Pakistan Army. On March 18, General Raja and Major General Rao Farman

Reluctant Fathers

Ali discussed the Operation at the GOC's office at Dhaka (Dhaka) cantonment. The full operation plan was a 16 Paragraphs Spread Over Five Pages.

General Farman briefed the operational principles and conditions for a successful outcome. Simultaneously, General Khadim Raja prepared for a military unit's deployment and assigned operation tasks to individual brigades. The military high command speculated that the Bengali soldiers might revolt during the operations. The command ordered that all Bengali soldiers must be disarmed before executing the Operation.

The command ordered all the political leadership must be arrested but must not be killed without proper justification—the high command bypassed President Yahya Khan. No operational briefing was given to the President. On March 20, General Abdul Hamid Khan and Lt. General Tikka Khan reviewed the searchlight operation plan in the Flagstaff House. Breaking the chain of command under military rules is a serious offense. In this case, General Abdul Hamid Khan is a de facto President.

However, after a thorough review of the plan, General Abdul Hamid Khan revised the plan. He ordered not to immediately disarm the regular Bengali army but approved the disarmament of the EPR, armed police, and other paramilitaries. President Yahya Khan ordered not to arrest Awami League leaders during a meeting with him. The original plan was amended. And the high command order to execute the amended plan to all military commanders.

The Searchlight Operation started at the military time 0100 on March 26,971 in Dhaka. It was a military surgical operation that minimizes innocent civilian casualties and maximizes the losses of the enemies. The

87

primary target was Dhaka University. The secondary target was Hindu Minority, and the third was Awami goons.

As I said, this was a military surgical operation meaning that all the military commanders had enough intelligence about their subjects. It was not like some Bangladeshi Bengali believed a random killing of innocent Bengalis. Those who have military officer training know it was a military operation, not like target killing like goons. However, the human mistake does happen in everything.

Declaration of Independence

According to the authentic information about the official declaration of Independence, a junior Pakistan army officer declared in Chittagong. He was later named Major Zia by the Pakistan military. On March 27, 1971, Major Zia declared Bangladesh's Independence on the radio, as I heard on YouTube. However, most of the Bengali believe Mujib had declared the Independence of Bangladesh on March 7th, 1971.

In Jackson Heights, NY, a Bengali told me that his relative so and so. Took the declaration of Independence from Mujib on March 25 and gave it to Zia. Logically speaking, how that would be possible. Before Arrest, Mujib was surrounded by the students' leaders and Awami leaders. The Operation was top secret; even President Yahya did not know about the searchlight operation. Dhaka to Chittagong approximately 152 miles. In 1971, the roads were not well developed as of today. The military started the Operation at 0100 military times. It means to see and shoot the target. And Major Zia was a very sincere, brave, and professional junior Army officer. How Mujib knew about him and trusted him to declare the Independence of Bangladesh.

Reluctant Fathers

These all are fictitious made-up stories. I do not care who declares Independence, but the history should be authentic.

The lies and fabricated stories are everywhere, literate to illiterate, about the declaration of Independence of Bangladesh. As reported by the news media, Major Zia is rightfully credited for his decisive action to declare "Independence officially." He clearly said, "I, Major Ziaur Rahman, Provincial Head of the government, do hereby declare that Independence of the People's Republic of Bangladesh." As a result of this declaration, he became the first President of Bangladesh in political science.

Bangladesh Government

On April 17, 1971, at a village alongside the India-Bangladesh border, Baidyanathtala, in Kushtia district (currently Meherpur district), was on East Pakistan soil first Bangladesh Government was formed by the main Agartala Conspirator Tajuddin Ahmad. Before creating the Government, Tazuddin Ahmed confirmed with Golok Bihari Majumder D.G BSF.

In 1971, Golok Bihari Majumder played the crucial role as a fundamental military backup for the Mujibnagar Government against the Pakistani military from day one. Majumder, the then D.G BSF (Eastern Command), was also the primary mouthpiece for communicating with the Indian Prime-Minister and Defense Minister for the Bangladesh interim-government of Bangladesh. During 71war., Majumder was the primary source for information, coordinator in management of the affairs at the ground level operation by guerilla fighters. Without Golok Bihari Majumder, Bangladesh's liberation war was impossible.

Professor Yusuf Ali read the proclamation of Bangladesh Independence, drafted by Amir-ul Islam and reviewed by Subrata Roy Chowdhury, a lawyer at the Calcutta High Court. On April 17, 1971, Answering a journalist question during the ceremony, Tajuddin named the Mujibnagar after Sheikh Mujibur Rahman's name. Later the government-in-exile came to be popularly known as the Mujibnagar Government. Mujibnagar was abandoned hurriedly after the ceremony's oath as participants feared a raid by the Pakistani military. In Kolkata, the Government Headquarter was in exile for the rest of the war—briefly at a house on Ballygunge Circular Road and then at 8 Theatre Road.

The War

Dhaka University students started the 71 war in the middle of 1970 by intensifying violence, loot, and target killing in Dhaka. The mobs of Dhaka took full advantage of the anarchy. The lawlessness confused the military intelligence and pro-Pakistani elements. It was complicated to make a political assessment in a 23 years old politically unstable country. That led to miscalculated political decisions by the Generals.

Major Zia formally declared war in Chittagong on March 27, 1971. This textual declaration meaning of "declaration of Independence Bangladesh." Originally, Serajul Alam Khan declared the Independence of Bangladesh while addressing a few students in the middle of 1970 and instructed them to create a Bangladeshi flag.

Serajul Alam Khan was known as a mysterious man. His move during 1968-71 was unpredictable. Frequently changing his movement to avoid Pakistani military arrest and well-connected with the Indian counterpart.

Reluctant Fathers

Mukti Bahini

After creating the interim Government Of Bangladesh in Calcutta, my blood relative (according to family tradition nephew and English tradition 2nd cousin) was promoted as War General. He was entirely responsible for oversight of the war leadership and gathering all the details of the strategic operations. He was getting obnoxious with the Indian defense ministry with their interference to his day-to-day task. He felt the entire war was fought by Indian generals, not him. He is just for show. A few times, he discussed the matter with the Mukti Bahini sector commanders. They told him, " Sir, there is no U-Turn." "We are in a situation where there is no return except Pakistan's military withdrawal or handover power." "The fight must continue, or millions will die, including us." He realized the war was imposed on us by India. He remained as war General until 1972 before making him Defense Minister.

He did not participate in the surrender ceremony. He knew he would play as a showcase. As he was a former Pakistani colonel, he felt sad in his heart that his former colleagues surrendered under Indian Generals, their former foe.

Mujib Bahini

Mujib Bahini was a well-known gang to Dhaka residents during 1948-1966; after the 1946 riot, Mujib knew Dhaka would be Pakistan's Capital. Therefore, after Partition, he created his place in Dhaka by using Huseyn Shaheed Suhrawardy's name.

During the 71 war, a Mujib Bahini by the Mujib devotees' was designed to fight a guerilla war against the

Pakistani military. I have met with Abdur Razzaq two times in my lifetime. One time, I met with him in Sylhet Hotel Kashmir to listen to his 71 accounts. I paid for his hotel room. The second time I met with him in Astoria, NY, by that time he was a minister. As I always said, "Bengalis are big fat liars" finding the truth from them extremely difficult. Mujib Bahini's participation in the war was highly disputed.

Serajul Alam Khan went to meet with India's Prime-Minister, Ms. Indira Gandhi. She turned him down. She said, " Indian Defense Ministry. " It means Ms. Indira Gandhi did not want to recognize Mujib Bahini or implied it is a terrorist group.

Qader Bahini

Qader Bahini was entirely under Qader Siddiqi's leadership, supported by Golok Bihari Majumder; It was only a non-former Pakistani military-trained guerrilla group. Qader Bahini committed massive war crimes after the Pakistani military surrender.

Pro-Pakistani Elements

Bengali often uses Razakar as a curse. Razakar, a volunteering force, was created during June's month by the pro-Pakistani element counterproductive to Mukti Bahini. Lieutenant General Tikka Khan was under pressure from the Muslim League to train volunteers to fight and defend the country; otherwise, the pocket will fight everywhere. General Tikka Khan always assured Muslim Leaguers that the Pakistan Army could defeat three India together and "Laughed."

Reluctant Fathers

However, on 2 August 1971 by the Governor of East Pakistan, Lieutenant General Tikka Khan. The Ordinance approved the creation of a voluntary force to be trained and equipped by the Provincial Government. He promised, "the weapons are coming from the USA." It was a big lie. Until this day, no weapon shipment reached East Pakistan from the USA.

Al-Badr

Al-Badr was a powerful pro-Pakistani Mujaheed group. The name was chosen from the Ghazwat Badr because the war between East Pakistan and India was first in 1971. West Pakistan fought against India a couple of times before. Ghazwat Badr was the first war between Muslims and Musrik in Al Madinah.

As one of my first cousins was the prominent commander of Al-Badr, I have heard first-hand stories from his own words during a family conversation. However, publicly discussing Al-Badr stories was a big no-no. As a kid, I did not know why it was a very secretive discussion. When I was growing up, I fully understood why not to talk about Al-Badr.

To make history straight, my cousin passed his BS degree in 1968 in Sylhet. He was applying for Chittagong University to finish his MS. His mother told him to take a break for a year or two to stay with her. As he was the only son, he agreed. During the 1970 election, he was in Chittagong. My auntie told me in the bedtime story that After March 27, she heard somebody eating in the kitchen in the middle of the night. She wakes up to see who it is. She saw my cousin washing plates to eat food. She asked, " why did you come without sending me a letter. I would

93

have cooked for you, good for you. He told my auntie, "Gaddar, Major Declared war on us."

She was asking him with her shaken body, " what will happen now?". He said, " what else, jihad against Musrik and Munafiq". She started crying. She said, " you are my only son." He said, " see me in Jannah if I die, or make Dua become a Ghazi. Allah will listen to your Dua" Staying with her for a couple of days, he left the village. Yes, Allah listened to my auntie Dua. My cousin did more than a dozen successive operations against the Indian military and Mukti Bahini. He never got injured during the fight. The Mujib government never arrested him or the Hasina government. He died with his honor. His intention was pure.

In April 1971, In Sylhet, he organized pro-Pakistani and Islamic-minded youngsters aged between 19-25, meaning college students under the banner of Al-Badr. Some retired army soldiers and officers join the group. My father heard about it. One day he found him in a Masjid in Sylhet. He warned him not to kill innocent people and our relatives. He promised he would not. The Al-Badr members increased to nearly two hundred thousand from Sylhet, Chittagong, and Comilla Districts, but there were not enough weapons for all the members. Al-Badr's primary source of weapon was buying from the black market. Black market weapons are from the Indian black market. Loot from the Indian Army or Mukti Bahini. In other words, Al-Bard fought against India with Indian weapons.

The Pakistan government was afraid of the international community labeling it as a terrorist-sponsoring state or did not have enough weapon supplies to support Al-Badr, or military ego got hurt by fearing that the volunteering group defeated the Pro-Indian terrorists and the Indian Army.

Al-Shams

I do not know the origin of the Al-Shams group. But I heard that Shams is a person's name, whether it's a nickname of the person or a real name of the person I do not know. I heard Al-Shams mainly recruited from Pakistan Democratic Party, Muslim League (Jinnah), National Awami Party, Pakistan Socialist party. They outnumbered approximately a hundred thousand. They were funding their guerrilla war expense from their party fund: no foreign help or Pakistan government help.

Islamic Jihad or Jundiin Muhammed

Islamic Jihad mainly recruited from qawmi madrasa students. Mostly poor and orphan students. Their funding was actually from collecting donations from ordinary Muslim families. They were not well-trained organized fighters. After the war, a few of them got killed by the Mukti Bahini, and some of them received threats not to talk about Pakistan in Bangladesh. They went back to their Madrasa. In Bangladesh, most people show pity on them. That's why they were saved from revenge killing. End of the day, everyone knew Pakistan was created in Muslim Nationalism. Everyone understood that qawmi madrasa students were fighting emotionally, not politically.

Peace Committee

The peace committee was one of the fragile unity between pro-Pakistani parties. The objective was to prevent extrajudicial killing by the Pakistani military in East Pakistan and repatriation for pro-Indian terrorists. The

Reluctant Fathers

parties were involved with the Peace Committee; they were Nizam-e-Islam, Jamaat Islami, Pakistan Muslim League, And Pakistan Democratic Party. Under two names: Nagorik Shanti Committee (Citizen's Peace Committee) and Shanti Committee (Peace Committee)

As a Muslim League Leader, my father was Shanti Committee (Peace Committee) standing committee Chairman. The name differs based on your party affiliations. Islamic minded political parties prefer the name Nagorik Shanti Committee (Citizen's Peace Committee)

After verifying the accused's identity with their family identity, the peace committee's functionality was to release accused pro-Indian terrorists from Pakistani Military custody. And advising their parents to warn their son to return from misguidance and stop associating with Indians. That's about it.

Finally, the 1971 war was conducted by the defect Pakistan military junior officers and financed by the Indian Defense Ministry. India entirely conducted the war operation financially and by military logistics. There is no evidence of Bengali nationalist fine line organized conventional or guerrilla war strategy against Pakistan. The 1971 war victory credit goes to one hundred percent to the Indian military—nobody else in the world.

India's secret war in Bangladesh would have served little purpose without a conventional, disciplined military force to secure a decisive victory — a lesson of the utility and limitations of sub-conventional warfare that ought to be closely studied today by the several states that rely on these tactics. (The Hindu, 12-26-2011)

Reluctant Fathers

Bangladesh

Who named Bangladesh? This question many people asked me throughout my life. I am originally from Sylhet. Sylhet was the capital of Assam until the thirteen century. Historically, King Gour Govinda was the king of Sylhet. His official language was **Nagri,** and **his religious** language was Sanskrit because Mantras are in Sanskrit. There were thirty tribal kings under his jurisdiction. As some Bangladeshi Bengali aggressively argued that Sylhet also Bengali seems that they will make Sylheti (Assami) as Bengali by their own lips service and aggressively poor behavior, they will make Sylhet as Bengali. All Bangladeshi Bengalis do not like to recognize that Sylhet joined Pakistan as Muslim nationalists by a referendum in 1946.

Historically, Sylhet was the Hindu Kingdom that consisted of thirty petty kings and never gave allegiance to the Sultanate of Bengal. Sylheti culture, language, and politics were different from indigenous Bengali. Why am I using the word indigenous? Several times, Sylhet had the burden of the influx of migration; those migrants were called "Bengal." I used to sympathize with Bengali because I saw a daily basis Bengali bullied in Sylhet.

My dad was a Muslim League leader. In 1971, my father was a peace committee Chairman. Bengali people curse Razakars, al-Badr, and al-shams; that's why I always sympathized with them. I firmly believe the idea of Pakistan imposed on Bengali. Of course, East Bengali, Sylheti, Arakani so-called Muslim politicians voted in favor of Pakistan's creation, but most Bengali was not agreed.

Muslim League assumed the so-called Muslim in Bengal like the idea of Muslim Country Pakistan. However, disgrace Jinnah made the situation worse. If Jinnah were a sincere Muslim politician, he would have been preparing for Pakistan's Constitutional Islamic Republic because the Muslim League stand by the two-nation theory since 1906. March 23, 1940, Muslim League passed a resolution to create Pakistan; at that time, the enthusiastic Bengali did not directly oppose Pakistan's creation.

However, Creation of Bangladesh, Jinnah is 100% responsible. Jinnah always opposed Pakistan's idea and emphasized Indian Federalism He was fighting for his 14 points under the Muslim League political banner. In early 1946, Jinnah telegraphed Huseyn Shaheed Suhrawardy that the British Government might not agree with creating a new country. Huseyn Shaheed Suhrawardy telegraphed back to Jinnah to keep negotiating with the British negotiators and know that all the options are on the table except the division of Bengal.

In mid-1946, Jinnah suddenly declared direction action without consulting with the Muslim League cabinet members. My educated guess and authentic information suggest that I.B. Officer in the night told Jinnah that if he wants to make a History, he has to incite the violence between Muslims and Hindu. The direct action is known in history as the 1946 riots.

In 1947, Jinnah could have a civil political discussion with the Muslim League cabinet members. Instead, he made his own decision based on the

Reluctant Fathers

negotiations with the British Counterpart. The weakness Muslim League cabinet members had the unpredictable Hindu Muslim bloodshed and refusal of the British Government to create Pakistan. That's why Jinnah found the opportunity to play a monkey business between Muslim League and the British Government.

Suppose Jinnah was sincere to create Pakistan, two Pakistan, East, and West and federalized it as the Islamic Republic of United Pakistan. Mosquito brain Jinnah was an opportunist, not a politician.

My research showed Ishwar Chandra was originally named Bangladesh, and in 1966, Indian agents capitalized it. Bangladesh is a reality. According to Indian history, East Pakistan is a blink of an eye. We all need to forget about 1947-1971 and let Bangladesh find its own.

Bangladesh Economy

Pre-1947, the East Bengal economy was in the hands of more than fifteen thousand Hindu Zamindars. Their Banking reserve was in Calcutta. They heavily industrialized Calcutta but nothing in Dhaka or Sylhet. First, Calcutta was British India's capital for nearly one hundred fifty years. Secondly, the provincial capital of Bengal.

During the partition negotiation between Lord Mountbatten and Jinnah, Lord Mountbatten was under pressure from England's Bank not to give Calcutta to Pakistan. Last two hundred years, London was a direct business partner with Calcutta. The high volumes of financial transactions between Calcutta and London were at stake. That's why they were mountains of pressure on Lord Mountbatten not to handover Calcutta to Pakistan.

Reluctant Fathers

Lord Mountbatten lured Jinnah to make him a Governor-General, a title Jinnah was obsessed with since childhood. Jinnah accepts the deal without understanding the financial consequences. The transfer of power was in Karachi, a small town compared to Calcutta, Lahore, or Dhaka. Lord Mountbatten played the same trick as Lord Clive.

On the day of the transfer of power, almost all seniors Muslim League were shocked. They received the information through a telegraph that Lord Mountbatten and Jinnah agreed on the creation of Pakistan. There were no details given for the preparation for the partition. Lord Mountbatten played a psychological game with Jinnah.

On August 14, 1947, East Bengal left on an unknown horizon. No one knew the exact situation. Lord Mountbatten left a map on the hand of Jinnah. Once again, Muslims in Bengal were deceived by another Mir. Jafar.

Muslim League was not prepared for this financial challenge at all. However, the Bank of Lahore set up the Pakistan Banking system and created cash flow into the economy at the beginning of 1948. As fifteen thousand Hindu Zamindars converted their assets into Indian Rupees, that's a sound alarm to the Muslims. All the political parties in East Bengal unanimously voted for the land-reform act.

In 1950 land-reform acts did not benefit the poor people as a thought in East Bengal. The former Hindu Zamindars' employees took full advantage of the new law. They were well aware of Zamindars' assets and connected with the legal professional, making it easy for them to take those assets.

Reluctant Fathers

During 1948-1958, Pakistan was under ideological gridlock. The Muslim Nationalists dominated Sylhet, Dhaka, Chittagong, and Comilla districts. North and South Bengal were overwhelmed by the socialists and communists. On the other hand, West Pakistan was filled with tribal and religious tension between Shi, Sunni, Hanifi, and Barelvi. There was no political or economic settlement at this time in Pakistan. Pakistan was growing by the wealthy families' private investment. In the Jute Factories, Sugar Factories, Paper Mills, and textiles.

In 1958 Military took over, President Ayub Khan laid a master plan to lead Pakistan in 21 century. He built a good relationship with Muslim Leaguers and wealthy families known as 22 families. His vision was before 1980, Pakistan would defeat Japan in the economy. Between 1958-66, Pakistan was growing on the fast track of economy and education that shocked the world.

The basic Democracy plan created nearly five thousand small towns and made millions of businesses and jobs. The Basic Democracy Union Presidency helped to build primary schools in the remote area. The blunder mistake of the 1965 war was disastrous for United Pakistan. It did affect East Pakistan's economy significantly.

With the ongoing violence between 1967-1971, Pakistan's economy was unsustainable. Pakistan's economy was in turmoil; wealthy families began to convert the asset to US dollars and UK pounds.

During 1972-75, Bengalis were dying of starvation. Two Muslim Leaders helped Bengalis with foods King Faisal bin Abdulaziz and Sheikh Zayed bin Sultan Al Nahyan

Reluctant Fathers

In 1977-78, my father and Shah Azizur Rahman, with many other Muslim Leaguers, met few times to discuss the Muslim League's future. My father said, "it is naïve to believe that East Pakistan and West Pakistan will ever become a United Pakistan." "It is better to make Bangladesh Muslim League.". However, in a restaurant, my father told Shah Azizur Rahman. " Muslim League does not have future in this country." " If Zia invites you to join with him, join." " use your political experience and knowledge for these poor people Sake of Allah." He looked at my father with a surprise. He said, Lal Saab, you are the boss and a sincere senior leader. I respect your opinion and will think about it."

President Zia invited Shah Azizur Rahman to join with BNP. He accepted the offer to join BNP. President Zia made him a labor minister. He made some robust labor reforms to boost the economy. He advised President Zia to built a stable relationship with Muslim countries.

President Zia, King Khalid bin Abdulaziz, and Sheikh Zayed bin Sultan Al Nahyan signed a kafil system to send Bangladeshi to Gulf Countries; the scheme's architect was Shah Azizur Rahman. Shah Azizur Rahman. Reshape the foreign policy of Bangladesh. Today, Bangladesh is a product of political genius Shah Azizur Rahman., not Mujib.

In the late 90s, I met the former finance minister Mohammad Saifur Rahman. He and I talked in a restaurant for a couple of hours in NYC. When we were both deep into the economic discussion., he asked me what can be done differently. I called the waiter for the bill. The waiter came with the account. I took my wallet to pay the bill. He said, "NO." But I paid. I asked him, "Sir, what did you see? He asked "where"?. I said, "sir, you are an economist, and you have seen nothing." I explained to him. I said, "first, we came. We sat on the chairs. A waiter came and asked for the order of food. No one knows why we came here in this world, but the waiter indirectly told us to spend money in order to sit in here. That's the modern economy.

The economy Thinking about a human as a consumer. Or a worker that's called economy. Secondly, I explained to him, "I expensed, and you saved." Socially it's honorary hospitality but economically "save and expense." In Bangladesh, the economy needs lots of foreign reserves and cut the import. Increase the export. He smiled and said, "Mirasdari blood." Thank you! I learned a lot.

Conclusion

In conclusion, I have experienced the Bengali nationalists' abusive behaviors toward Muslim activists in Bangladesh. The mistake was already made in 1906, 1946, and 1971. These mistakes cannot be corrected by returning to the dates. Cursing Razaker, Al-Badr and Al-Shams will not do any good to the country. I assume it is a pretext to take sympathy of the Bengali.

The country is heavily suffering from injustices, loot, rape, murder, fraud, thieves, land invasion—political instability. It is time for the new generation to rethink. Should they stick with Bengali and Pakistani hatred or move forward as unified Bangladeshi.

In reality, Bangladesh is an internationally recognized country and member of the United Nations (U.N.). It is insane to believe Bangladesh and Pakistan will ever be united. It is overpopulated and condensed at 160 million people, is one of the world's poorest countries. The Government of Bangladesh cannot afford to engage in a conventional war against any external enemies. The country should create a confederacy union with the neighboring countries, especially with India.

The alleviating poverty dream of the past, in this current geopolitical and overpopulation crisis. Bangladesh needs a master plan to tackle the internal political, social, economic, religious, educational disturbances.

The Government of Bangladesh must prioritize eliminating criminalistic culture to ensure all Bangladesh citizens' safety and security, disregarding political, religious affiliation, and Social hierarchy, and restore the ethical culture. That will increase the reputation of the country and lure investors into pouring in in the economic sectors. The quality of the life of people will habitually improve with the flow of financial vibration.

Further reading:

Caste: The Origins of Our Discontents

By Isabel Wilkerson

Publisher: Random House (August 4, 2020)

India's External Intelligence: Secrets of Research and Analysis Wing RAW

by V.K. Maj. Gen. Singh

Manas Publications (July 30, 2007)

India Wins Freedom

Maulana Abul Kalam Azad

Publisher: Sangam Books Ltd; 1st edition (December 1, 1998)

Jinnah: India, Partition, Independence

By Jaswant Singh

Publisher: Oxford University Press; 1st edition (February 28, 2010)

Conflict Diplomacy: the U.S. and the Birth of Bangladesh Pakistan Divide

By Jaswant Singh

Publisher: Rupa Publications India (February 1, 2008)

Democracy and the Challenge of development
A study of politics and military intervention in Bangladesh
By Moudud Ahmed,
Publisher The University Press Limited

Reluctant Fathers

Red Crescent Building, 114 Motijiheel c/o P.O Box 2611, Dhaka 1000, Bangladesh

Bengali Politics Documents of the Raj, Editors, Enyetur Rahim, Joyce L. Rahim

Publisher The University Press Limited

Red Crescent Building, 114 Motijiheel c/o P.O Box 2611, Dhaka 1000, Bangladesh

The Betrayal of East Pakistan

A. A. K. Niazi

Oxford University Press, Feb 24, 2000

Islamic Economics, Theory and Practices, A comparative Study

M.A. Manan

Printed 1991

Sh. Muhammed Asaraf, Publishers, Booksellers & Export, 7 Aibak Road, New Anarkali, Lahore, Pakistan

Websites:

https://sourcebooks.fordham.edu/india/1617englandindies.asp

https://en.wikipedia.org/wiki/Main_Page y a community of volunteer contributors, anyone can change the information from Wikipedia.

Made in the USA
Coppell, TX
22 May 2021